428

Living LANGUAGE

INVESTIGATING TALK

Susan Cockcroft

Hodder Murray

A MEMBER OF THE HODDER HEADLINE GROUP

D0258236

Acknowledgements

Copyright Text:

'One Deaf Poet' by Walter Nash from *Latterdays in Sundry Places* © Walter Nash; Transcripts 1, 3 and 14 reproduced with permission from Ann Henderson; Transcript 2 reproduced with permission from Natasha Law; Transcript 4 reproduced with permission from Jonathan Flannigan; Transcript 5 cited from Cheepen and Monaghen (1990); Transcripts 6 and 8 reproduced with permission from Rosalind Preston; Transcript 9 reproduced with permission from Christine Fletcher; Transcripts 10, 11 and 12 reproduced with permission from Stephen Jephson; Transcript 13 from Snow (1977) cited in *Children's Conversation* by Michael McTear (1985) Blackwell; Transcript 16 from *Analysing Talk* by David Langford (1994) Macmillan; Transcript 17 from *Language, Society and the Elderly* by Nikolas Coupland, Justine Coupland and Howard Giles (1991) Blackwell; Transcripts 20, 21, 22 and 23 reproduced with permission from James Hurdis; Transcripts 24 and 25 reproduced with permission from Neil Wright; Transcript 26 cited by Geoff Thomson in 'Linking Context and Systems' at 8th Euro-International Systemic Function Workshop, Nottingham 1996; Transcript 27 from *Framing in Discourse* by Deborah Tannen (ed) (1993) Oxford University Press; Transcripts 28 and 29 reproduced with permission from Amber Brown; Transcript 30 cited by Ruqaiya Hasan in 'Speaking with Reference to Context' at 8th Euro-International Systemic Function Workshop, Nottingham 1996; Transcript 31 from 'Defendant resistance to power and control in court' by Sandra Harris, cited in *Working with Language: A Multidisciplinary Consideration of Language Use in Work Contexts* by Hywel Coleman (ed) (1989) Mouton de Gruyter; Transcripts 32 and 33 reproduced with permission from NEAB; Transcript 34 cited in Drew (1994); Transcript 35, reproduced with permission from Margaret Walker; Transcript 36 reproduced with permission from Michael Macken; Transcript 37 student transcribed data from *Any Questions*, BBC Radio 4; Transcript 38 reproduced with permission from Alex Lanterna; Transcript 39 from *Coronation Street* (1998) reproduced with permission from Granada Television; Transcript 40 from *The Archers* (1998) reproduced with permission from BBC Radio 4; Transcript 41 from *Blind Date* (5/12/98) reproduced with permission from Granada Television; Extract from *Absolutely Fabulous* reproduced with permission from BBC Books; Extract from 'Brontëburgers' in *Up to You Porky: The Victoria Wood Sketch Book* (1985) Methuen; Transcript 42 from *Eddie Izzard Unrepeatable* (1994) reproduced with permission from Ella Communications Ltd/Polygram Video Ltd; Transcript 43 from BBC News 27/9/98; Transcript 44 from BBC Weather Forecast 27/9/98; Transcript 45 reproduced with permission from BBC; Transcript 46 from Michael Halliday lecture at the 25th International Systemic Functional Summer School and Congress, Cardiff July 1998; Transcripts 47, 48 and 49 reproduced with permission from Karen Dell; Transcript 50 from *Women Talk* by Jennifer Coates (1996) Blackwell; Transcripts 51 and 52 from *Women, Men and Politeness* by Janet Holmes (1995) Longman.

Every effort has been made to trace copyright holders of material reproduced in this book. Any rights not acknowledged will be acknowledged in subsequent printings if notice is given to the publisher.

Orders: please contact Bookpoint Ltd, 130 Milton Park, Abingdon, Oxon OX14 4TD. Telephone: (44) 01235 827720, Fax: (44) 01235 400454. Lines are open from 9.00–5.00, Monday to Saturday, with a 24 hour message answering service. You can also order through our website www.hoddereducation.co.uk

British Library Cataloguing in Publication Data

A catalogue entry for this title is available from The British Library

ISBN–13: 978 0 340 73086 7

First published 1999
Impression number   10   9   8
Year   2007

Cover photo from The Ronald Grant Archive
Typeset by Fakenham Photosetting Limited, Fakenham, Norfolk NR21 8NL
Printed in Malta for Hodder Murray, a division of Hodder Education, 338 Euston Road, London NW1 3BH.

Contents

1 The Importance of Spoken Language

It's good to talk!

Talking is what makes us human. Animals, insects, birds, even plants successfully communicate through a rich variety of means – but only humans can articulate their most complex ideas, feelings and needs by means of the vast, global range of sound systems, which we call *language*. This book will explore this extraordinary phenomenon from a range of perspectives and in a variety of ways.

Historically, written language has always been valued more highly than spoken language because of its relative permanence. Pictures, hieroglyphics, pictograms, characters, ideograms and alphabet letters have been used by human beings to record and relay information to each other since the days of cave paintings and drawings scratched on rock. Today, symbols or *graphemes* can provide a 'permanent' visual representation of the sound systems and meanings of languages. (Even so, not all languages today have written forms, presumably because they are not needed by the various speakers.)

Great advances in the study of spoken language this century have been made possible by the tape recorder and the dictaphone. Recordings of a vast range of naturally occurring spoken languages can be made and (providing permission is gained), the resulting transcriptions analysed. Not only are linguists, dictionary makers and scholars interested in these recordings – tapes of police interviews, transcribed statements, even 'bugged' conversations are often used as crucial evidence in court. Indeed, forensic linguistics is one of the most fascinating new branches of linguistic study today.

Another major advance in the re-evaluation of spoken language has been the development of the computer, with its capacity for storage, classification and analysis of information. Texts and/or tape recordings of naturally occurring talk can be transcribed and fed into powerful computers, and the resulting database analysed to find out about everything from grammatical usage to syntactic patterns, from slang usage and frequency of idioms to monitoring change over time, *from* semantic *to* phonological. These databases or *corpora* (the singular version is *corpus*) are frequently established in universities, often in association with publishers of dictionaries. Important examples of corpora include the Collins-Birmingham University International Language Database (COBUILD) (written and spoken) and the Cambridge-Nottingham Corpus of Discourse in English (CANCODE), at the University of Nottingham, part of the Cambridge International Corpus (spoken).

Remarkable changes in our interest in and attitude towards spoken language are happening now. Instead of talk being regarded as ephemeral and of little value compared with written language (for example, in fields like law, government and politics, business, science, academia etc), we learn from corpus linguistics that spoken language is an equally complex and valuable system of communication. The grammar is different, the lexis is different, the structures are different – are its functions different? Scientists, neurologists and linguists are making equally important advances in the field of *artificial intelligence* – that is, teaching computers to match the immeasurable range of activities the human brain is capable of performing, including speech. Artificially produced voices still sound rather Dalek-like, but voice-activated and voice-responsive computers are very much on their way. (We shall be looking at how this works, at the processes of *acoustic modelling* (sounds we produce) and *linguistic modelling* (sounds interpreted as words) in the next chapter.)

The structure of this book

The rest of Chapter 1 begins by introducing some of the theories and explanations about how talking began, put forward by a range of linguists, archaeologists and biologists. This will be followed by an overview and summary of recent thinking about the areas of the human brain responsible for language (particularly spoken language), with some comments on children's talking in the family. Following this, we will look briefly at speech production and speech dysfunction (stammering, memory loss and memory lapse) and how therapy can help. Then we shall address the main focus of the book by inquiring how speakers acquire individual skills and idiosyncrasies (*idiolect*) and what makes us successful talkers. This leads us to some of the key questions to be investigated in detail in the book. How do people talk to each other today, to friends and family, at work, on the telephone, in public, to a large or small audience? How do their listeners respond? What makes a good listener? Do people really listen to each other (or to themselves) talking? What do we make of talk around us all the time? Why do we sometimes misunderstand each other, and how do we put things right?

The rest of the book should help you to investigate and find some answers to these questions. Chapter 2 focuses on the sounds, structures and functions of talk. Chapters 3, 4 and 5 investigate a wide range of examples of talk: public and private; planned and unplanned. Chapter 6 concludes the book with a case study of the effects of one particular sociolinguistic variable – *gender* – on talk and talking.

So who were the first talkers?

In Mary Shelley's *Frankenstein* (1818), the monster created by Frankenstein recalls how he learnt human language from the loving family he secretly observed. This is what he says:

> By degree I made a discovery of still greater moment. I found that these people [*the family the monster was hiding from*] possessed a method of communicating their experience and feelings to one another by articulate sounds . . .. This was indeed a godlike science, and I ardently desired to become acquainted with it. But I was baffled in every attempt . . ..Their pronunciation was quick; and the words they uttered, not having any apparent connexion with visible objects, I was unable to discover any clue by which I could unravel the mystery of their reference. By great application . . . I discovered the names that were given to some of the most familiar objects of discourse: I learnt and applied the words *fire, milk, bread* and *wood*.
>
> (*Frankenstein*, World's Classics edition, p89)

Shelley presents the monster created by her hero, Frankenstein, as a prototype of an early human. A modern writer, William Golding, imagines how early humans may have talked in his novel about Neanderthal people, *The Inheritors* (1965). In *The Tempest* (1611), Shakespeare creates a strange figure named Caliban, part human, part savage, taught to speak by the magician Prospero. The following exchange shows Shakespeare presenting the acquisition of language as a double-edged skill:

> *Prospero* . . . I pitied thee
> Took pains to make thee speak, taught thee each hour
> One thing or other. When thou didst not, savage,
> Know thine own meaning, but would gabble like
> A thing most brutish, I endowed thy purposes
> With words that made them known.
>
> *Caliban* You taught me language, and my profit on't
> Is, I know how to curse. The red plague rid you
> For learning me your language.
>
> (*The Tempest* Act 1, Scene 2, lines 354–65)

However brutishly Caliban behaved, Prospero had given him a remarkable gift – an ability to communicate his meanings through speech. What is important about this extract and all the other examples is that they confirm that language is *the marker for membership of human society.*

ACTIVITY 1

Task: to investigate basic modes of communication

Working in pairs, take turns to communicate a piece of information on a previously agreed topic using:

1 gestures only

2 vowels only
3 consonants only
4 vowels with gestures
5 consonants with gestures

Which was most/least successful? Discuss your findings with the group.

Out of Africa

When we start to think about the first speaking human, the stereotype might be someone like Caliban or even Fred Flintstone. But were the earliest humans really like this? How did they live and speak?

Twentieth-century archaeologists have given us a clearer picture of early humans, and of their primate forebears who lived in Africa some 6 million years ago. Jean Aitchison in *The Seeds of Speech* (1996) describes how 4 million years ago, our human ancestors called *hominids* split off from the other primate groups (*pangids* and *panids*, ancestors of gorillas and chimps respectively). This may have happened because a series of violent earthquakes in East Africa broke apart the earth's surface and created the Great Rift Valley. We are descended from these early hominids: from *homo habilis* (2 million years ago) and from *homo erectus* (1 to ½ million years ago). It is thought that language was first used by modern man (*homo sapiens*) between 200,000 and 100,000 years ago, when the physiology of the human vocal tract had developed sufficiently. It seems likely that some kind of vocalised communication took place between hominids up to a million years earlier. To use spoken language, humans had to develop the right shaped jaw, the right length of tongue, the right resonating cavities in the skull and a sufficiently mature nervous system. Archaeological evidence of these physical developments enabled linguists to propose the dates above.

Early humans were social beings and lived in groups, and it seems likely that they would have used vocalised sound in a variety of ways: to socialise with each other (cf grooming rituals in primates); to communicate danger (the African vervet monkey can warn other monkeys of danger from snakes, eagles or lions by differentiated calls); to work together co-operatively (eg hunting or fishing). According to Steven Pinker in *The Language Instinct* (1994) *homo habilis* skulls 2 to 2½ million years old show signs of wrinkling in the left hemisphere of the brain, suggesting a potential for language. *Homo erectus* moved out of Africa into what we now call Europe, China and Indonesia between 1½ and ½ million years ago. These humans may well have used some form of language, since they were able to control fire and use symmetrical, well-crafted stone hand-axes (Pinker, 353). *Homo sapiens*, our direct ancestors, came 'out of Africa' only 75,000 years ago, bringing with them language, hunting and farming tools and possibly religious and cultural traditions. They talked and walked their way into Asia and Australasia, the Middle East and then into southern Europe, where magnificent cave paintings (dated 35,000 BC) have been discovered. Five thousand years later, the most adventurous *homo sapiens* crossed from the Eastern European landmass over the Bering Straits and down through North America into South America.

Travelling talkers

How can we know all this? Possible links between the peoples of Africa, Europe, the Americas, and those of Asia and Australasia are the focus of much research. One theorist has identified DNA-based genetic links between peoples who *once* lived in the same geographical areas and *now* speak widely differing languages. There are significant similarities in form and meaning (*cognates*) between certain languages, suggesting a single *earlier* language as a common ancestor. Another theorist identifies common language features which may be shared between widely separated and seemingly different languages.

It certainly makes sense that as humans settled, moved on (leaving behind the refuse of their domestic life for modern archaeologists to discover), they would talk and tell stories about hunting, about travel, about dangers. Over thousands of years, different ways of talking or 'languages' must have evolved among different groups in different places. If the brain of *homo sapiens* is specially adapted for language, as Chomsky argues, early humans may have developed 'languages' as they gave *names* to parts of the body, to the landscape around them, to the basic elements of life, and to sensations (hand, head; rock, sand; fire, water, meat; hot, cold). With the realisation that things can have **names**, all language begins. Each tribal group of *homo sapiens* might describe their world slightly differently, using different sound combinations to make words, organising them into different patterns or syntactic structures, and applying different rules of language or grammar. Groups of *homo sapiens* living at great distances from other groups might create seemingly different languages, but all would have to be able to: *name*, to express *difference between oneself and others*, to describe *more than one-ness*, to be able to talk about *action*.

It is possible that language family groupings today (Indo-European, Uralic, Afro-Asiatic, Caucasian, Dravidian, Austro-Asiatic and Amerind) still reflect the migration patterns and languages of *homo sapiens*. Unique languages like Euskara (spoken in the Basque region of Spain) or Etruscan (spoken in pre-Roman Italy and still not fully understood) tell us that the story of human languages is far from being known. The earliest of human languages have vanished and been subsumed into the languages spoken today – of which there are between 4,000 and 10,000, depending on whether you count dialects and other closely related languages. The future survival of many of these languages is a matter for concern as the last speakers die off, English continues its inexorable rise to dominant world language status, and the destruction of tribal life in distant parts leads to unknown language losses. *Homo sapiens* appears to be endangering its own richly diverse linguistic heritage.

ACTIVITY 2

Task: to investigate similarities between disparate languages

1 Look at the following cognates (words with the same meaning in different languages):

- *brother* (English)
- *phrater* (Greek)
- *frater* (Latin)
- *bratre* (Old Slavic)
- *brathirr* (Old Irish)
- *bhrater* (Sanskrit).

What are the main points of similarity?

2 Find cognates for the following words from any languages you know:
milk, fire, water, rock, hot, cold, tree, hand, foot, head.

For each word, list the cognates (identifying each language source), place them in groupings if appropriate, and present a written or oral report on your findings.

Talking in the family

Jean Aitchison suggested that early humans had to develop what she called the *naming insight* in order to acquire language; young humans today (whatever their language) start to name objects and people around them as they begin to acquire language. Because of this link between early humans and children today, we shall look at early stages of children's talking to help us to imagine how *homo sapiens* may have learned to talk about the world they lived in.

If you want to learn more about the different theories concerning language acquisition, you should read *Language Acquisition* (Frank Myszor, 1999), another book in this series. What triggers this process seems to be a combination of social and functional factors. The child has a need, and wishes to communicate this need to the care-givers. Michael Halliday's functional theory of language acquisition convincingly demonstrates that as the child's needs grow more complex, so does her language, as it reflects her developing understanding of the physical and social world. By the age of two and a half, most talking children can:

1 use intonation to ask questions
2 use turn-taking skills
3 point to objects or people (deictic or pointing words and/or gestures)
4 give commands
5 express personal feelings and needs
6 give information
7 name things and people
8 recognise patterns in language structures and make analogies (syntax and grammar)
9 show understanding of the passage of time (tense)
10 talk about something that is not actually present.

In the following transcripts children aged three, four and six are talking with adults. At the end of each extract a commentary identifies interesting features.

Transcript 1

*Child **L** (female) aged 3 and a half talking to researcher **A***

L   look
A   are you gonna build something
L   yeah (2.0) I'm gonna build a tractor
A   let me watch hey
L   what
A   can I watch you building
L   erm (1.0) there (3.0) and then he's gonna sleep in there
A   yeah
L   and (1.0) and then he's gonna sleep in a bed
A   in a bed
L   yeah
A   yeah
L   and he's just been to work
A   has he what work has he done
L   he's done builder work
A   has he
L   yeah
A   what did he build
L   he build a (2) zebra
A   a what
L   a zebra
A   a zebra
L   yeah
A   how can you build a zebra

(Source: Ann Henderson)

COMMENTARY   L uses deictic word 'there'; understands past time 'he build'; can name something not present 'a zebra'.

Transcript 2

*Child **M** (male) aged 3 looking at a picture book with **D** (father)*

If you are using the *Living Language Cassette*, you will find Transcript 2 on it, as 'Investigating Talk Extract 1'. The recording also includes the 'passage omitted'. You can use this to practice your own transcribing skills.

D   now what's happening here
M   they're they're cov … they're um they're burying daddy
D   they are burying daddy with all the blooming sand aren't they
M   yes
D   I think she's happy about that don't you
M   yes but he but Thomas used to bury me
D   did he
M   yes
D   that's not very nice of him is it
M   yes it is
D   oh you like it do you
M   yes
D   is it good fun
M   mmh

D now then what
M and I buried him too
D did you
M mmh
D what can you see on that page
M they're they're playing on a bit of the beach
D yeah
M bit of it
D can you see other things as well
M that's a ice-cream thing
D ice-cream where you buy ice-creams from
M mmm and horse
D rocking horse isn't it
M yes no it's not it's a horse to put pennies in
D oh it's a horse oh that's a clever boy where you put the pennies in it you have a
       ride on it you clever boy

(Source: Natasha Law)

COMMENTARY M is able to use tense and aspect correctly 'they're playing', 'used to bury',
'I buried'; deictic words 'that's a icecream thing'; negative usage 'no it's not'.

Transcript 3

*Child **C** (male) aged 6 talking to his mother **M***

C do you know what
M (1.0) what
C (3.0) I found (.) a fossil today
M really
C I mean a tooth
M a tooth
C yeah
M wasn't one of yours was it
C no (2.0) no it was off a dinosaur
M a dinosaur where in school
C no not inside
M outside
C erm
M in the play area
C yeah I saw a hole and then I looked in it and then I saw a (.) saw one
M a tooth
C yeah (.) and then I digged in with my finger (1.0) and then I saw one
M are you sure it just wasn't a piece of stone
C (.) no
M why did you think it was a tooth
C (3.0) because it was
M (2.0) well sounds interesting enough to me

(Source: Ann Henderson)

COMMENTARY M is able to talk about something he's only heard about: 'dinosaur', 'fossil',
using words from the appropriate semantic field. He is able to discuss the
proposition that the stone is a dinosaur's tooth, and narrate the process of
discovering it. He has developed skill in structuring his narrative: 'I saw . . .
and then I looked . . . and then I digged'.

Transcript 4

*Child **J** (female) age 4 talking to her teacher Mrs **A** and another adult Mrs **P***

J Mrs A— my ulcer hurted that's why I came in
A OK go and sit down
J shall I get a wet paper towel
A what have you been doing to make it hurt
J don't know shall I have a drink
A yes does that feel better
J no
A have you been playing outside
J been playing and it hurts you got lots of paper haven't you you've got an apple
my dad likes the skin on apples what are these
A I'm cutting out sticky spots for a game who have you been playing with outside
J playing with Charlie justed played together then it hurted it so hurts I like these
spots pink and green are my favourite colours
A what are you going to do this afternoon
J I don't know what I'm doing today I have to do what my teacher says
A you should really be outside playing now shouldn't you
J no I want to stay in because it hurts Daddy says I can have some cream tonight
Mrs P did Daddy say I can have some cream now
P no he said you can't have any on until tonight now let me take you outside
J oh I want to stop in with Mrs A—

(Source: Jonathan Flannigan)

COMMENTARY J uses questions confidently: 'shall I have a drink', including tag questions:
'haven't you' as well as complex syntactic structures: 'I want to stay in
because it hurts'; 'I have to do what my teacher says'.

These transcripts of children talking provide evidence of the remarkable
developments in children's spoken skills over a relatively short period, and
confirm the centrality of talk to their cognitive as well as social maturation.

ACTIVITY 3

**Task: to investigate selected aspects of
children's language development**

Asking permission first, record a conversation
between children (aged 2–5) and other children
or adults (in as relaxed an environment as
possible) in which they tell each other, or the
adult(s), a made-up story. Write a detailed
commentary on the language of each child,
identifying features from the list on page 6.

Speech production and speech dysfunction

Speech Production

We are able to *talk to each other* because: we can produce sounds with our
vocal system; we can organise sounds into words in the brain; we can hear

sounds through our auditory system; and we can interpret what other people say with the brain. When people *listen to us talking*, exactly the same process occurs. Conversation is in every sense two-way! In the diagram below (adapted from Aitchison, 1996) you can see the actual structure of the brain. Language processing takes place in many areas of the brain, but it seems likely that the posterior (rear) section often called Wernicke's area controls the reception and comprehension of language (Speech Interpreter) and the anterior (front) section in the left hemisphere (side) of the brain, called Broca's area, controls the production and expressive functions of language (Speech Organiser). Neurologists and psycholinguists have suggested that different parts of Broca's area are responsible for how we sequence words (word order), how we make associations between words (collocations or groups of words), how we express condition or possibility (if . . . then . . .) and how we articulate sounds.

Figure 1

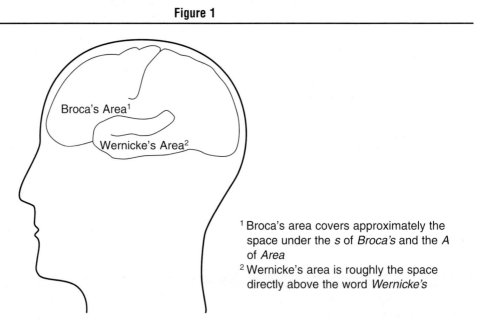

[1] Broca's area covers approximately the space under the *s* of *Broca's* and the *A* of *Area*
[2] Wernicke's area is roughly the space directly above the word *Wernicke's*

When we speak, how do we choose our words? How do we 'know' how to pronounce the language we are speaking so we can be understood? In *Words in the Mind: An Introduction to the Mental Lexicon* (1987), Jean Aitchison proposes a model of the mental 'dictionary' we draw on when we speak. This lexicon contains between 50,000–250,000 words or *units*. Each unit or word is like a coin with detachable sides: meaning and word-class on one side, and sound structures on the reverse. Different words can be linked together if they share similar characteristics with either side of another unit or 'coin'. The lexicon is composed of two overlapping networks: the *meaning and word-class network* and the *sound structure/phonological network*. These networks are linked to a third component, a '*lexical tool-kit*' which contains procedures for making up *new* words. These networks have firm links but flexible boundaries, and are adapted for rapid production of words, and identification of sounds heard and understood. We access these networks in the lexicon as we listen to and understand what people are saying to us. Once accessed, the networks will activate more words than are needed, seek other connections, experiment with morphemes – 'on the go' continually as they search, select, dismiss – until the search narrows and the final choice of word and sound is made. This activation of these network links 'within the mental lexicon and in adjacent components such as syntax and memory' is 'potentially limitless' says Aitchison (1996, pp 198–99). Such hugely complex, yet seemingly effortless processes in the brain enable us a) to find the words we want and b) to know how to say them.

Speech dysfunction

If something goes wrong with any of these systems and processes, if the networks fail to activate because of physical or psychological problems, acquired or developmental, the result is *language dysfunction*. A road accident, a stroke, a neurological problem, malformation of the speech organs – all of these can lead to problems with talking, reading or writing, at any age. Yet everyone experiences mild speech dysfunction, and 'slips of the tongue' are so commonplace we hardly notice them. According to Aitchison, these are either *assemblage* or *selection errors* and each can affect the processing of the meaning, word-class and phonological networks. For example, 'par cark' for 'car park'; 'muxed ip' for 'mixed up' are phonological assemblage errors. 'Allegory' for 'alligator', 'arthuritis' for 'arthritis' or saying 'Mary' when you mean 'Jane' are different sorts of selection error. Memory problems (short and long term) can also affect anyone at different stages in their life.

Figure 2

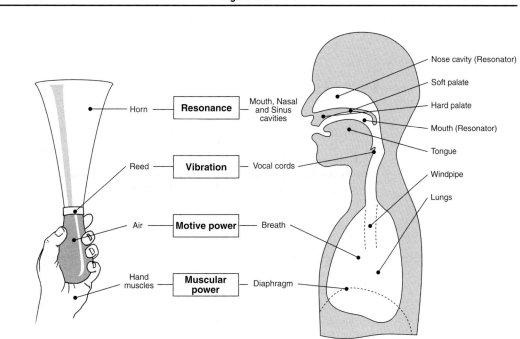

Speech dysfunction means that spoken communication has been affected by serious and abnormal errors in the processing networks, producing developmental or acquired aphasia or language loss. These can range from physical problems (deafness or cleft palate) causing stuttering and poor pronunciation, to developmental problems (eg dyslexia or 'word-blindness') to the effects of injury or stroke (cerebro-vascular accident). For example, a stroke victim might lose their *word-retrieval skills* in a particular semantic field: on being shown an orange, the patient might be unable to name it, yet be perfectly able to name a banana, pear, or apple. Similarly a patient might use bizarre word associations, false synonyms or nonsense words if *semantic processing* was faulty. A problem in *processing syntax* might lead to confused word order; a difficulty with *word-class processing* might mean the patient used no verbs or pronouns. For people with these kind of language processing difficulties and their carers, talking is often painfully frustrating. Speech therapists, however, have evolved a variety of strategies to reconnect lost network links; one example is *melodic information therapy*, which means using familiar word/music combinations to trigger syntactic, semantic or phonological patterns in the patient's memory. Encouragingly, the success rate in enabling people to talk satisfactorily again after a stroke is between 50% and 75%.

ACTIVITY 4

Task: to investigate some examples of speech dysfunction

Ask around (tactfully) among your family and friends to see if they have knowledge or experience of adults or children with speech difficulties. If possible, arrange to talk to the person involved, or their family, about the particular kind of speech dysfunction and how it was treated. Ensuring that permission has been given and that your subject is not named, write up your notes into a short report (approximately 300–500 words).

Creating an idiolect

As talking humans, we all have our own *idiolect* or unique way of using spoken language (our written usage is described as 'style'). This individual idiolect reflects physical characteristics such as voice quality, pitch and tone, as well as inherited vocal features, such as a tendency to lisp, or sensitivity to high or low frequency sound. Childhood experience of language may affect its pace of development, and the acquisition of confidence in using language. Gender is another significant factor in developing the individual idiolect in the context of family, school and the world at large. Social and economic status, peer group pressure, occupational experience (parental and own) together with education and cultural background all make a difference to the way we talk; so does our ethnic background and where we live. Even body language can affect our spoken skills. Good talkers who communicate their individual viewpoint well tend to maximise strong points such as a clear voice, an ability to look people in the eye, a moderate use of non-fluency features, a respect for people's personal space. People can change aspects of their idiolect – the classic example is Margaret Thatcher, a former Conservative Prime Minister, who lowered her vocal pitch, allegedly to gain more powerful masculine tones. Others may wish to lose their 'unfashionable' regional accent and acquire modified Received Pronunciation (RP), allegedly acceptable everywhere. People who normally use taboo language at every point will temporarily drop it if the occasion (eg interview, family funeral) warrants; others who would not normally use taboo language bring it out in certain circumstances (eg football match). These examples of 'tinkering' with an individual idiolect are exceptions; our patterns of language are 'set' very early on, and most of us relish the way our spoken language reflects our uniqueness as individuals.

ACTIVITY 5

Task: to investigate examples of individual idiolects

Select two or three people you know who have different accents. Ask each to talk to you informally on tape about a topic they feel comfortable with (eg early school days, a special family occasion, a funny or embarrassing experience, a day out etc). Aim for about 3–5 minutes taped talk from each person. Then listen carefully (probably three or four times) to each narrative. You should then be sufficiently familiar with each speaker to identify specific

features of their idiolect. Make notes under the following headings for each speaker:

- *vocal quality* (include pitch, tone, intonation variation, volume, pace)
- *pronunciation* (any regional variants in vowels, dipthongs, ellipted consonants)
- *lexical choice* (include any dialect or regional terms, job-related vocabulary, slang, taboo usage)
- use of *hesitations, fillers, false starts.*

Compare your findings with others in your group and report back to your class.

Talking with a purpose

The famous linguist, Michael Halliday, once described language as a 'social semiotic' – that is, a system of signs or symbols used by human beings to communicate with each other. Speech is the most important among many modes of human communication; others include: body language (paralinguistics), communication by touch (proxemics), eye contact (gaze) which all function together to enhance the power of the spoken word.

Why do we talk?

We talk because we have *needs* to communicate (seeking information, asking for help, expressing feelings, describing people, objects or places, giving explanations, instructions or commands, socialising, persuading people).

Talking is nothing if not functional! Halliday's theory of metafunctions offers a convincing theory about the way language works whether spoken or written. The *ideational metafunction* relates to the world we talk about, live in and react with; the *interpersonal metafunction* refers to the way we relate to each other; and the *textual metafunction* means the mode of language used for communication.

Who we do we talk to?

We talk to people we know, people we don't know at all; we talk to ourselves, we talk in our sleep; we talk to pets, we talk to toy rabbits; we talk in public and in private; sometimes we know in advance what we're going to say, sometimes we have no idea – 'How do I know what I think, till I see what I say?' is a not unfamiliar remark. We talk one-to-one, to a few friends, to a large group, to a public meeting, to a radio audience, to a television audience. We talk face to face, on the telephone, on voice mail or the answer phone, to the voice-activated computer, to the internet (even e-mail is a kind of talking).

Where do we talk? And for what particular purpose?

The context and purpose or function of talking will vary enormously, and will have a significant effect on all aspects of the dialogue or exchange, from lexical choice to use of interactional devices, frequency of non-fluency features, length of utterance and number of interruptions or overlaps. We constantly shift or accommodate our language choices (including accent) in conversation, to fit the context and purpose, often without realising it. Linguists differentiate between *transactional* spoken language (used to obtain goods and services, such as buying a pair of jeans) and *interpersonal* spoken language (used for socialising, in the common room or club, for example). Interestingly, some interactions can be both. An obvious example is talking to the doctor: in the consulting room the talk is transactional; meeting him or her at a party or in the supermarket the conversation is interpersonal.

Are we all good at talking?

This may seem a ridiculous question – of course everyone is good at this first of skills, aren't they? On reflection, is this actually true? Many people find that putting their ideas (and especially their feelings) into words is incredibly difficult; hesitation and other non-fluency features dominate their conversation. Others may say a lot – never stop talking, it seems – but communicate very little, especially anything personal. Others use talking as an instrument of power, to dominate and destroy people, though not always deliberately. Some people lie, prevaricate, and use their language skills to manipulate others and exploit their verbal vulnerability. Some people are terrible listeners and always have to chip in, anticipate or even rephrase the other speaker's words. Worst of all, and most demoralising, is the person who never, never listens. They may allow you to speak, but everything you say will be referred back to their own experience. You are then quite literally a sounding board.

What makes a conversation 'successful'?

A simple response to this might be that an exchange has succeeded if all participants have achieved their primary purpose; if every speaker felt able to communicate ideas without inappropriate interruption; and if there was co-operation between participants. A more detailed analysis of successful conversation might investigate the use of politeness strategies; terms of address; facework; management of social distance and social solidarity; conversational maxims and implicatures. Let's look at a brief summary of each.

Why is politeness important when we talk to each other?

Politeness means showing respect for the person you're talking to, whether the exchange is formal or informal. We need to respect the other person's face needs.

Face needs

Positive face needs means that we want to be liked and approved of (hence the way we use greetings, compliments and appropriate terms of address). *Negative face needs* means that we wrap up unpleasant requests or orders by using hedges ('it's *sort of* difficult but . . .') and apologies ('I'm sorry but would you mind if . . .'), thus avoiding face-threatening behaviour. We need to respect the relative status, social distance and social solidarity between participants in a conversation, and be responsive to the social and cultural context (don't call an interviewer by her first name unless she asks you to; don't use taboo language with a head teacher; don't call your best friend by their full name if they prefer a nickname etc). E. Goffman also introduces the idea of *footing* (1981) in connection with the way people align themselves to what they are saying (in other words, their stance).

Your footing in talking to a university admissions tutor, for example, is that of would-be participant and you would adjust your language appropriately.

Positive and negative politeness

Brown and Levinson in *Politeness* (1987) describe in detail positive and negative politeness in conversation. *Positive politeness* means that you claim common ground with other speakers and convey your assumption that all participants wish to be co-operative. Some positive politeness strategies are:

1 pay attention to the other speaker(s) (show interest, sympathy, approval)
2 seek agreement (choose safe topics)
3 avoid disagreement (pretend to agree, use white lies, hedge your own opinions)
4 presuppose or assert common ground
5 make jokes
6 assume or assert agreement between each other
  (and there are more!).

Negative politeness means that you are indirect, don't presume or assume anything, don't force your point or impinge on the other person. Some negative politeness strategies are:

1 be indirect
2 question and hedge
3 be pessimistic
4 give deference
5 be apologetic
6 go on record as being indebted etc.

ACTIVITY 6

Task: to identify politeness strategies in use in the public domain

Record a radio or television one-to-one interview. Select and transcribe a short extract (2–3 minutes only); then analyse your data to see what kind of politeness strategies are being used.

ACTIVITY 7

Task: to examine the way politeness strategies can be used in drama to create character

Record an episode of a radio or television soap opera. Listen carefully to the taped episode (remember that it is scripted and not naturally occurring conversation). Select at least one major character (eg Grant in *Eastenders)* and explore how the scripted use of politeness strategies and conversation maxims reflects his or her 'character'.

Conversational maxims

In 1975 H.P. Grice proposed four basic conversational maxims as criteria for successful conversation:

1 be relevant (*maxim of relevance*)
2 be truthful and have enough evidence for what you say (*maxim of quality*)
3 speak appropriately – don't talk too much or too little (*maxim of quantity*)
4 speak in a clear, coherent and orderly way (*maxim of manner*).

Conversational implicatures are inferences based on the normal assumption that the conversational maxims are being followed. Thus if someone says 'I'm hungry!' a reply might be 'There's the Cat and Fiddle', the inference (or implicature) being that the Cat and Fiddle sells food, is nearby and is open, fulfilling the maxims of quality and relevance.

ACTIVITY 8

Task: to identify conversational maxims in use

Record *either* a conversation with friends or between family members *or* in a work situation.

Listen carefully to the tape several times (unless you have time to transcribe it). Decide whether the speakers *fulfil* or *flout* the conversational maxims.

Thus **successful talking** is when the conversational maxims and politeness strategies are working effectively; unsuccessful talking is when the maxims are flouted, the facework is threatening and the appropriate politeness strategies are ignored. To demonstrate these 'in action' we'll finish this chapter by analysing politeness strategies in a conversational transcript.

Transcript 5

Hosts C and J are greeting guests G and T

C [ ] did you get lost then
G [ ] hallo
T [ ] [*laughs*]
G [ ] no we didn't what we did however encounter was an accident on the road
C [ ] not to you
G   oh no no no no [*inaudible*] there were thousands of cars sort of piled up sort of miles back on the road that goes from Watford to
C   ooohhh
G   St Albans
C   oh my God
G   [*inaudible; offers bottle of wine*]
C   how nice ... oh I I'm a [*inaudible*]
G [ ] it cost two pounds and seven p
T [ ] [*laugh*]
C   well I'm sure we'll give it
G [ ] [*laugh*]
C   the um consideration it deserves

G [ ] oh what a charmer
ALL [*laugh*]

(Cheepen and Monaghen, 1990, p171)

COMMENTARY

In this short extract we can see that **C** greets the guests with a question about their lateness whilst simultaneously **G** greets **C** 'hello' (phatic communion) and then gives a clear explanation of why they were late (maxims of *quality, quantity* and *relevance*). Although there is no direct apology, the detailed explanation implies apology (*negative politeness strategy*). **C** responds to **G**'s explanation with concern (*conversational implicature*: the excuse is acceptable). **G** introduces another topic by presenting a gift (bottle of wine), which **C** accepts with appreciation (*positive politeness strategy*). **G** uses another politeness strategy to comment on the price of the wine, at which **T** laughs (either another positive politeness strategy or embarrassment). Depending when the recording took place **G**'s comment on the price is either a positive or negative politeness strategy (ie the wine was expensive or the wine was cheap). **C** then uses two positive politeness strategies by implying future enjoyment of the wine together (**G** laughs – positive politeness strategy), and by making a joke which plays on the previous comment about the cost of the wine. **G** responds with a further ironic joke (positive politeness strategy) at which all laugh. This shared laughter confirms that the impoliteness of **G** and **T** in arriving late has been forgiven. What role does footing play here?

2 Sounds, Structures, Functions and Features

Sounds – noises off . . . and on

If you stop reading now and listen – what can you hear? Someone doing carpentry, the hum of the word processor, a distant aeroplane, children shouting? If we are fortunate enough to hear well, we have a huge advantage as communicators; the personal imprisonment imposed by gradual loss of hearing for someone who loves language (and especially talking) is articulated below by this scholar poet:

ONE DEAF POET

Small garden – voices gossiping on their stems,
the chaffinch's pebble of song, are lost to me;
my ears are closed to intricate device;
somewhere aloft, the lark is dropping stitches,
but I miss the click of the needles. Music shrinks.
Listening hard, I grasp only the gross
purport of the notes; the delicate
harmonics flutter briefly and elude me.

Audition's edifice crumbles. Bricks and bats,
wreckages of dry consonants, high vowels,
tumble out of my belfry, and the chimes
ring tinnily for vespers; grumpy, I lurk
suspiciously in the neighbourhoods of whispers.
'You have to shout', visitors are instructed.
The more they shout the less I am informed;
shouting is amplifying formlessness.

How common talk distorts to comedy!
'Another slice of bread' reaches me as

An 'overflight of dread', and 'aftermath'
as 'have to bath'. I hear a garbled text
by Peter Snug, filtered though Wonderland:
affable salesmen say 'a marbler's aid
offers a cistern with your healing problem'.
Cisterns and marbles will not heal me much.

But what of that? Neighbours, I am a poet,
I am an auditorium to myself.
Hooped in the strict confinement of my skull
elated wings of rhythm lunge and dart;
rustles within shape the sonorities
of forms, measures, sounds in permutations
and patterned mazes, seeking, endless, endless,
a resurrection and the hope of heaven.
I nurture words of comfort that may yet
foster the Word. I wait in isolation
in this dark temple, murmuring 'Speak, Lord,
and thy servant will hear'.
   I am not deaf, after all.

WALTER NASH

In this section we shall look briefly at the production, transmission and reception of speech via the human vocal-auditory system. **Phonetics** is the study of these processes: *articulatory phonetics* analyses the way sounds are *produced* by the vocal organs; *acoustic phonetics* analyses the physical *properties* of speech sounds; *auditory phonetics* analyses the way speech sounds are *received*. **Phonology** is the study of the sound systems of a particular language. **Phonemes** are the individual units of sound within a particular language.

We can divide the sounds humans produce (whatever the language) into several groups – consonants, vowels, diphthongs and less common sounds (such as the *ch* sound in Dutch *gracht* meaning 'canal', or the click sounds in Xhosa). How you *produce* the sound makes all the difference: in most languages air is expelled from or drawn into the lungs, and depending on its route out of or into the mouth, different sounds are made. It also makes a difference whether the vocal chords are being vibrated or not (eg in English, 'b' is voiced, 'p' is unvoiced).

Consonants

There are 24 consonants in English. They are produced by air being expelled at the front of the mouth with the positioning of the lips, teeth, tongue and alveolar ridge (the bone behind the teeth) changing the sound produced. These include consonants made with the lips (*bi-labial* /p/, /b/, /m/); consonants made with lips and teeth (*labio-dental* /f/, /v/ and *dental* /th/); consonants produced by the tongue on the ridge behind the teeth (*alveolar* /t/, /s/, /n/ and *palato-alveolar* /sh/, /j/); and consonants produced by the tongue and hard palate (*velar* /k/, /g/, /j/, /ch/, /ng/). There are a few unusual consonants that sound like vowels (*approximants* /w/, /y/), or that pass through the mouth unaltered (*aspirate* /h/).

David Crystal identifies four ways in which these consonants are produced: by complete closure of the vocal tract, followed by release (*plosives* eg /p/, /t/, /g/; *nasals* eg /m/, /n/, /ng/; *affricates* eg /ch/ and /j/); by intermittent closure (eg *trilled* /r/ and single tap on uvula or alveolar ridge, depending on regional pronunciation); by partial closure – air passes on either side of tongue (eg *lateral* /l/); and narrowing, where two vocal organs are so close that air can be heard passing between them (*fricatives* eg /f/, /v/, /h/, and *sibilants* /s/, /z/, /sh/).

Vowels

There are 20 vowels in English. They also pass through the mouth cavity relatively unrestricted; the difference between vowel sounds is determined by the way we hold our mouth, whether the sound is sustained (long vowel) or of brief duration (short vowel). The mouth is widest for /a/ and the narrowest for /o/. The other parts of the mouth that move, apart from the lips, are the tongue and the soft palate (uvula), and vowels are produced at the front, centre and back of the vocal cavity. English vowels can be *monophthongs* (single pure vowel /a/, /e/), *diphthongs* (two vowels together eg 'hope', 'hate') and *triphthongs* (three vowel qualities eg 'player', 'fire', 'tower'). Vowel variation shows up particularly clearly in regional accents – eg the famous Northern flat /a/, as opposed to the Southern long vowel in 'bath', 'grass'.

Figure 3

The International Phonetic Alphabet

The consonant sounds of English are:

/p/	as in *part*	/f/	as in *food*	/h/	as in *has*
/b/	as in *but*	/v/	as in *voice*	/m/	as in *mat*
/t/	as in *too*	/θ/	as in *thing*	/n/	as in *not*
/d/	as in *did*	/ð/	as in *this*	/ŋ/	as in *long*
/k/	as in *kiss*	/s/	as in *see*	/l/	as in *let*
/g/	as in *get*	/z/	as in *zoo*	/r/	as in *red*
/tʃ/	as in *chin*	/ʃ/	as in *she*	/j/	as in *yes*
/dʒ/	as in *joke*	/ʒ/	as in *measure*	/w/	as in *will*

The vowel sounds of English are:

(long vowels)		(short vowels)		(diphthongs)	
/iː/	as in *each*	/ɪ/	as in *it*	/eɪ/	as in *day*
/ɑː(r)/	as in *car*	/e/	as in *then*	/aɪ/	as in *by*
/ɔː(r)/	as in *more*	/æ/	as in *back*	/ɔɪ/	as in *boy*
/uː/	as in *too*	/ʌ/	as in *much*	/əʊ/	as in *no*
/ɜː(r)/	as in *word*	/ɒ/	as in *not*	/aʊ/	as in *now*
		/ʊ/	as in *put*	/ɪə(r)/	as in *near*
		/ə/	as in *again*	/eə(r)/	as in *there*
				/ʊə(r)/	as in *truer*

Why study the phonology of a language?

When we listen to a language we don't speak ourselves and don't understand, problems begin. The phonemes are different from English phonemes; the syllable and word boundaries (created by consonants and consonant clusters) are unrecognisable; the stress and intonation patterns are completely unfamiliar; and everyone talks too fast! The stream of sound rushes by us, until suddenly it stops – we have been asked a question. To respond is automatic – turn-taking is our earliest language experience – but how? In despair we resort to paralinguistics (facial expression, body language, gesture). Trying to communicate without sounds to convey meaning is at best, difficult and frustrating, and at worst, virtually impossible. Such an imagined but not unfamiliar scenario demonstrates the necessity of learning in detail about the sound systems, patterns and functions of any language, as well as its **prosody** (the *way* it is spoken; prosodic features include intonation, pitch, stress patterns, tone, volume and pace).

Understanding how spoken language works

The best way to understand this is to write down (transcribe) from a tape recording (transcribe) everything that has been said, and also note the hesitations and false starts. To get the most accurate results from naturally occurring language you need to ensure that the speakers are unaware of the recording. This avoids the *observer's paradox*, identified by William Labov in 1981. This is the distorting effect on people's spontaneous conversation if they know they are being recorded.

Making a transcription is time-consuming but rewarding. You should always allow much more time than you think you need, and to be safe, always make a duplicate tape and keep it labelled, dated and secure. Spoken language can be transcribed in *graphemes* (normal type) or in *phonetic symbols* (IPA – the International Phonetic Alphabet). If you transcribe in IPA you need to indicate word divisions by /.../ (eg /kat/ for 'cat'; /sez/ for 'says'; /fiːld/ for 'field'). Punctuation, apart from capitals for proper nouns and first person pronouns, is normally omitted. The following conventions are used whether you transcribe in graphemes or phonetics.

Pauses are be marked in seconds. (.) means a pause of indeterminate length; (4.0) for example means a four-second pause. If one speaker starts before the previous speaker has finished (*overlapping*) you can mark this with an elongated square bracket. In this book [ ] has been used. You can signal an immediate follow-up without overlap by = ; this is called *latching*. Boundaries in conversation (equivalent to commas, semi-colons, colons and full stops in punctuation) are often marked by / (minor boundary marker) and // (major boundary marker). It's also possible to represent intonation patterns in speech: ′ means rising tone; ‵ means falling tone; ˅ means falling/rising tones; and ^ means rising/falling tones.

ACTIVITY 9

Task: to transcribe an extract from a conversation in graphemes, marking specific features

Select a tape recording of conversation you have already made. Transcribe the first two minutes using normal graphemes, and mark the overlaps, pauses, latching and boundaries.

ACTIVITY 10

Task: to transcribe an extract from a conversation using phonetic symbols, and marking specific features

Select and transcribe a different two minutes of the same conversation in IPA, marking major and minor boundaries and falling and/or rising intonation.

The structures and functions of speech

What is discourse?

Talking is something most of us are rather good at and enjoy; our sophisticated interactional skills were established in early infancy. One of the most important skills we learnt was how to *structure* talk. The basic pattern of turn-taking is established long before vocalisation begins, whenever a baby smiles, moves her tongue, or wriggles arms, legs and body in response to her carer's voice. From this early structuring of interaction, the complex patterning of talk between humans develops. In this section we are going to examine in some detail the range of structures we all use as speakers of English. Our focus will be on examples of these structures being used to perform specific and various functions.

Throughout the book we shall be investigating a wide range of examples of spoken discourse. Simply defined, discourse means a unit of language in use larger than the individual sentence, clause or utterance. *Discourse analysis* is the linguistic analysis of naturally occurring connected spoken or written discourse (Stubbs, 1983); in other words the study of conversational exchange, dialogue and interaction between speakers in social contexts. This includes everything from casual conversation, interviews and court room language to answer-phone messages, classroom exchanges and transcribed texts such as parliamentary language.

Some important theories of discourse analysis include: **speech act** theory (Austin and Searle, 1969); **exchange structure** theory (Sinclair and Coulthard, 1975, 1992); **pragmatics** (Levinson, 1987); **ethnography of communication** (Hymes, 1974); **conversation analysis** (Sacks, Schegloff and Jefferson, 1973, 1984); **pragmatics** (Grice, 1975); and **frame and schema theory** (Minsky, 1974; Chase, 1977).

Discourse can be:

- either *transactional* or *interactional* (Brown and Yule, 1983). Transactional language is used when the participants are exchanging goods and services (eg going to buy some bread, going to see your lawyer), whereas interactional language is used when speakers are socialising
- structured according to the organisation of the spoken interaction only (structuralist or formalist view)
- structured according to the context of the spoken interaction (functionalist view). In other words, language has external (social) functions outside the linguistic systems of grammar, phonology and lexis etc.; these functions influence the way the discourse is structured
- described as utterances, thus combining the *formalist* emphasis on structure with the *functionalist* emphasis on language in use. Utterances are context-defined units of language, hence discourse as utterances 'sits at the intersection of structure and function' (Schriffrin, 1994, p41)
- structured according to the way it differentiates between *given* and *new*

information (Halliday, 1967). *Given* information is what we already know; *new* information is what we don't know. For example, this made-up conversation shows a mixture of given and new information (called a *cleft structure*):

A *Mum said you were very late last night* (given).

B *How did she know?* (request for more information).

A *It was Dad who told her* (new) *he had indigestion in the night and woke up* (new).

Some theoretical approaches to discourse analysis

Speech act theory

Speech act theory derives from the work of philosophers Austin (1962) and Searle (1969) whose central insight is that language *performs* communicative acts between speakers and listeners. These can convey information (*constative*) but perhaps more interestingly they can be *performative* (you are actually 'performing' the action as you speak; 'I welcome you ...' 'I demand that ...'). Performative utterances made by a speaker are called **illocutionary speech acts**; should they affect the listener in any way (persuade, annoy, amuse etc) they are called **perlocutionary speech acts**. Illocutionary speech acts have been divided by Searle into five types:

1 *representative* – when the speaker is committed to the truth of the proposition ('I believe', 'I conclude')
2 *directive* – when the speaker tries to get the listener to do something ('I request', 'I order')
3 *commissive* – when the speaker is committed to a course of action ('I guarantee', 'I swear')
4 *expressive* – the speaker expresses a personal attitude ('I deplore', 'I congratulate')
5 *declarative* – the speaker alters a situation by their action ('I dismiss you', 'I pronounce you man and wife').

According to **speech act theory**, successful speech acts must fulfil certain criteria, known as *felicity conditions* (although self-evident, people are not necessarily aware of them, and it is useful to identify possible reasons for conversations going wrong):

1 you must have *authority* to perform the speech act (promise or baptise or arrest someone)
2 you must perform the speech act *correctly* (welcome someone pleasantly; introduce a visitor appropriately)
3 you must perform the speech act *sincerely* (don't apologise if you're not sorry; don't pretend to believe or agree if you don't).

Not only do speakers assume that felicity conditions have been met when talking to each other, but they are also able to interpret indirect speech acts. For example, 'I'm boiling hot!' might be a simple statement of fact, but (depending on the context) it could mean something quite different ('please open the window', 'please fetch me a drink' or 'why did you tell me to wear my coat?').

What is useful about speech act theory is that it enables us to identify and label different communicative functions within utterances into separate segmented units which can be linked in sequence. Because individual speech acts can be illocutionary as well as perlocutionary, and can be indirect as well as direct, it is possible to start to map the optional and unpredictable nature of talk. Moreover, the identification of felicity conditions helps us to understand better what makes for successful conversation.

ACTIVITY 11

Task: to identify illocutionary and perlocutionary speech acts in everyday conversation

Listen to people talking casually and note the proportion of performative and constative speech acts in use. Then choose a short extract from your own transcribed data (or from a transcribed passage in this book), and identify as many examples as you can discover of illocutionary and perlocutionary speech acts, and conversational implicatures. Do the results from your own analysis reflect your experience of casual conversations?

Exchange structure theory

Exchange structure theory was developed by Coulthard, Sinclair and Brazil (1975 onwards) as a result of their investigation into interactions in school classrooms. They found that the transactional language of every lesson, whatever the subject, had the same interactional structure, with each move consisting of one or more speech acts. After an opening remark (framing move) such as 'Right', there was:

1 an initiating move, followed by
2 a response, followed by
3 teacher feedback/evaluation.

Figure 4

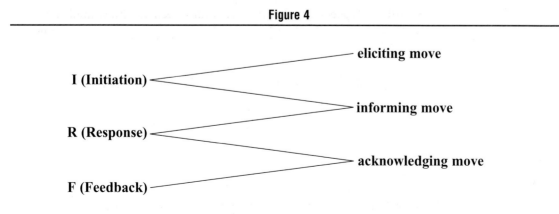

I (Initiation) ——— eliciting move

R (Response) ——— informing move

F (Feedback) ——— acknowledging move

Another way of putting it would be Move 1 – ask question, Move 2 – answer, Move 3 – comment; or yet another way of putting it, *initiation/response/evaluation*.

This *three-part exchange* represents what repeatedly happens in classroom interaction, with opening and closing framing moves providing exchange boundaries before the next three-part exchange begins. The following example demonstrates some more complex aspects of the exchange:

Teacher   Now let's get started. (*opening framing move*) Do you know the name of the capital of China? (*opening move or initiation elicits/informs*)
Pupil   Beijing (*response informs/acknowledges*)
Teacher   Good – do you know its old name? (*follow-up/evaluation/feedback acknowledges and elicits*) **or** Good – do you know its old name? (*follow-up/evaluation/feedback acknowledges and informs*)

The *two-part exchange* or *adjacency pair* is a familiar pattern of exchange, reminding us of our earliest interactions. Here are some variations on the basic pattern:

- question/answer ('What's the time?' / 'Six o'clock')
- inform/acknowledge ('The train's late again' / 'Yes, I'm really fed up')
- introduction/greeting ('John, this is Mary' / 'Hi John, how're you?')
- complain/excuse ('I've a splitting headache' / 'No wonder you lost your temper with him') etc.

Sometimes these adjacency pairs can be separated by an intervening utterance called an *insertion sequence* (eg 'How much did those jeans cost?' / 'Do you really want to know?' / 'Yes I do – don't be mean!' / 'Are you sure?' / 'Yes – I might get some for my birthday' / 'Well, they were a bargain – twenty-two quid').

David Brazil investigated the way intonation communicates meaning in the exchange, and argues for the *tone unit* rather than the clause or utterance as a structuring unit. (Each tone unit contains a *tonic segment* which is the syllable or word made prominent by the speaker's pitch and stress (eg 'Do you have the TIME'? / 'No I'm afraid my WATCH is broken'). An example of how tone unit structure can affect the communication of meaning appears in the following example, where the tone unit conveys the opposite meaning of the words ('He SAYS he's coming home soon' really means 'I don't believe he will').

What is useful about exchange structure theory is that it provides a flexible but structured model which can be applied to many *different* kinds of talking as well as classroom discourse.

ACTIVITY 12

Task: to investigate the use of three-part exchange structures in a lesson

Record (with permission) part or the whole of a lesson. Listen to the recording carefully, and select an extract which provides an example of three-part exchange structure. Identify each move in your example and describe its function. (You may also like to note how many examples of IRF (Initiation, Response, Feedback) exchange structure can be identified in the course of this, and other lessons.)

Narrative structure, frame theory and schema theory offer further structural approaches to discourse analysis. Each approach takes a different focus, and can provide differing insights.

Narrative structure theory

Labov's theory of **narrative structure** derives from his research into the effects of social deprivation on language (Labov, 1972). He sees narrative (which includes everything from oral history to telling jokes) as central to all forms of written and spoken language. Narrative can be defined as a unit of discourse with clear boundaries, linear structure, and recognisable stages in its development:

- abstract (*summary of the story*)
- orientation (*context in which the story takes place*)
- evaluation (*point of interest in the story*)
- narrative (*story telling*)
- result (*what finally happened*)
- coda (*signals the end*).

What is useful about narrative structure theory is that it recognises story telling as a discrete part of everyday spoken interaction with a unique capacity to hold the hearer's (or, in another context, the reader's) attention. Labov's identification of a story's structural features, and the differentiation between them (some features can be optional, others are obligatory) re-confirms the *integral nature of the relationship between form and function* in spoken language that we referred to earlier in this chapter.

ACTIVITY 13

Task: to apply narrative structure theory to a range of spoken narratives

1 Record one or all of the following:
- a friend telling you about something that happened recently
- someone telling a fairy story or nursery tale to a young child or group of children
- someone from a different age group telling a funny story.

2 Listen to the recording as many times as necessary and attempt to identify the individual stages of narrative described by Labov.

Frame theory

Frame theory is a theory about the structuring of discourse which argues that we use past experience to structure present usage. Goffman (1974) and Minsky (1974) were early exponents of frame theory, followed by Gumperz (1982). The latter's theory of conversational inference suggests that as we talk we pick up contextualisation cues (or frames) enabling us to recognise the situation and structure our responses appropriately. These mental frameworks help us to interpret the current situation and anticipate what is going to happen. Thus 'going to see the doctor', or 'attending a job interview' have particular frames leading to particular discourse structures.

Schema theory

Associated with frame theory is **schema theory**. The term *schema* means a mental model or knowledge structure in the memory, which has its own patterns of expectations, frames and assumptions. Deborah Tannen (1993) links frame theory with schema theory, and in a fascinating case study demonstrates how *conflicting frames* produced miscommunication between a paediatrician, a child patient, her mother, and the unseen video audience of fellow doctors. There was a medical register (*examination frame*); a friendly register (*paediatric consultation frame*); and a register appropriate for addressing the mother (*consultation frame*). Each frame creates and fulfils its own discourse expectations – unless there is a problem. Here, the doctor used medical register with the child.

Similarly, *mismatched schema* can also cause problems. The mother (mental schema: 'wheezing' means 'illness') was worried about the child's noisy breathing at night; the doctor (mental schema: 'wheezing signifies a specific medical problem which the child does not have') knew that the noisy breathing was normal for the child's condition. To reassure the mother the paediatrician had to adjust his schemas and needed to shift the frame from examination to consultation.

What is useful about frame and schema theory is that together they offer explanations of how people seem to 'know' how to interact in a variety of contexts, adjusting and shifting frameworks and schemas as required.

ACTIVITY 14

Task: to identify the use of frames and schema in naturally occurring spoken language

Listen to a television discussion programme like

Newsnight, Question Time or *The Late Show*. See if you can find any examples of the participants adjusting frames in the course of the discussion.

Pragmatics

Pragmatics is an approach to discourse analysis which focuses less on structures and more on the *contexts and purposes* of people talking to each other. A good description is provided by David Crystal: 'pragmatics studies the factors that govern our choice of language in social interaction and the effects of our choice on others'. The importance of Grice's conversational maxims of quality, quantity, relevance and manner has already been mentioned in Chapter 1, as well as his theory of implied meanings in talk (conversational implicatures). However, making sense of what we hear also depends on the context of the conversation, our experience of similar contexts and an assumption that the speaker's utterances are coherent, even if the conversational maxims are flouted. (Sometimes this is inevitable: a teacher needs to explain a topic in detail, so the maxim of quantity is overridden, or someone telling an elaborate shaggy dog story cheerfully flouts the maxims of relevance and quantity.) In both situations, communication remains successful because both speakers and hearers know *why* the maxims are being flouted, and the co-operative principle is sustained.

What is useful about pragmatics is that it takes into account everything about speakers and hearers, from the intentions of speakers to the effects of utterances on hearers, from their assumed 'knowledge, beliefs and presuppositions about the world' (Crystal) to the effect of situation or context and individual psychological factors upon what they say and how they interpret each other's talk.

ACTIVITY 15

Task: to see how closely people adhere to conversational maxims

Work in four groups of between four to six people. Agree on a conversation topic of general interest (holiday plans, weekend job, socialising, family events etc) and select a different conversational maxim for each group. Everyone should take a turn at being a non-participating observer in their group. The observer's task is to see whether the group's selected conversational maxim is being adhered to. The observer should take notes on each member's contribution to the conversation and report back to the group and to the class as a whole.

Conversation analysis

Conversation analysis is an approach to discourse analysis deriving from sociology and known as *ethnomethodology*. Sacks, Schlegoff and Jefferson (1978, 1984) are major theorists in the area. They focus on the way society affects spoken interaction, and propose that conversation itself constructs a sense of social order, because we all know the 'rules' of everyday conversation intuitively. In other words, naturally occurring spoken language has its own dynamic structure and rules deriving from social interaction, not from the 'rules' of grammar and syntax.

Conversation analysis investigates features in spoken language like turn-taking, adjacency pairs, speech markers indicating openings and closures, phatic communion, topic shifts, topic management, change of speaker, repair sequences, conversational inferences, contextualisation cues, sequencing of turns and turn transitions, politeness strategies and face saving devices. All these features can be found in successful conversation. If certain conversation 'rules' and expectations are *not* followed, then conversation is unsuccessful and miscommunication ensues. For example, linguists studying the effects of gender on language have found that men and women sometimes fail to understand each other because they follow different conversational 'rules', and hence misunderstand each other's meanings. Further miscommunication can occur if one or both participants misjudge or ignore the social situation (context).

What is useful about conversation analysis is that it recognises where the responsibility for the ordering, organisation and dynamic of talk lies – with the people doing the talking.

ACTIVITY 16

Task: to observe the way people talking adjust their talk to match other speakers and situations

Listen to a radio phone-in programme, and

note down examples of: phatic communion; opening and closing strategies; topic shifts; politeness strategies.

Ethnography of communication

Ethnography of communication is another sociological approach to discourse which describes the patterns of spoken communication as part of cultural knowledge and behaviour. Dell Hymes is a key theorist in the area. An alternative term for 'cultural knowledge' is 'communicative competence'. This means that the speakers of any given language will intuitively know its norms and variations, its cultural and linguistic constraints. Each speech act is part of a speech event which in turn is part of an sequenced interaction defined by the context and the participants in the discourse. For example, an ethnographic approach to discourse would use the findings about a particular speech act (such as questions) to learn about the nature of a specific speech event (interviews), basing this on cultural knowledge of the interview; in other words, an example of communicative competence. Whatever we say or do is meaningful only in the framework of our cultural knowledge, and the way in which we make sense out of our experience within our specific communities. A simple model of an interview between a sociologist and a respondent shows in its structure the shared cultural knowledge of both participants (the actual subject of their conversation is not directly relevant):

Sociologist:	question 1	(*seeks information*)
Respondent:	answer 1	(*provides information*)
Sociologist:	question 2	(*information check*)
Respondent:	answer 2	(*affirms information*)

Both people recognised what was expected of them in the exchange, and performed it.

What is useful about the ethnographical approach to discourse is that it locates speech events within the wider framework of the community where we all do our talking.

ACTIVITY 17

Task: to investigate examples of communicative competence

Record yourself interviewing an older friend or family member about their childhood, the kinds of games they used to play etc. Listen carefully to the recording several times.

1 Note down the ways in which your experience differs from theirs.
2 Assess the communicative competence of your interviewees, and the effectiveness of your own questioning to elicit information.

Smooth talking and not so smooth talking

In this last section of the chapter we shall be investigating fluency in talk, how it is achieved, and why problems of non-fluency can also emerge.

Spoken language is the mode or channel of communication which *makes real* the forms and functions of discourse by speakers' choices of lexis and grammar, as well as the discourse features appropriate to the context, participants and purpose. Below is a list of the characteristic features or realisations of spoken language, under the headings of grammar, lexis and discourse features.

Grammar

Grammar in the context of spoken language means the relationships between the words in an utterance, as well as the syntactic structures of an utterance. It is not based on sentences, which are the basis for the grammar of written language. There are different expectations and assumptions about grammatical usage in talk, and current research in corpus linguistics confirms that there are real differences between the grammar of written and spoken language.

Listed below are some examples of grammatical and syntactical features typical of spoken language:

- use of contracted verb forms eg '*Don't* be late!'; 'The *weather's* fine today'
- active rather than passive verbs eg 'The train *is running* late'; 'I *hate* waiting'
- frequent use of imperative and interrogative verb forms eg '*Fetch* the

post please'; '*Do you know* when the next train's due?'; '*Shall we go* into town this evening?'
- phrases (not clauses or sentences) and especially noun phrases, can stand as if they were complete utterances eg ' "Why were you so late?" "*Traffic jam*" '; ' "Where's the newspaper?" "*In the study*" '
- simple and usually short clauses, without much embedding in noun clause
- high proportion of co-ordinating clauses
- frequent use of 'and' as a continuation marker
- unusual clause constructions eg 'That film it's really brilliant'
- tendency to ellipt (cut out) grammatical features eg ' "Do you mind if we go home early?" "Of course not" ' (ie '*we don't mind*')
- use of deictics eg '*This* cake is yummy'; 'You take *this here*, and I'll put *that there*'.

Lexis or vocabulary

Lexis or vocabulary in spoken language is determined by the context, the purpose of the talk and the people who are talking. These factors will affect the register and the semantic field. Listed below are certain broad features which tend to characterise the vocabulary of spoken language:

- tendency to use more concrete, less abstract vocabulary
- tendency to use simpler and more generalised vocabulary
- low lexical density (number of words per utterance); higher proportion of function over content words
- context-determined lexical choice (ie determined by the topic of the talking)
- use of vague language such as fillers or hedging devices (eg 'er', 'erm', 'like', 'you know', 'sort of', 'whatsit', 'thingummyjig', 'thingummybob', 'oojah')
- use of terms of address eg 'Your Honour', 'Mum', 'Miss Smith', 'Jim', 'sir'
- frequent use of phatic language (polite expressions fulfilling the function of 'social lubrication') particularly in casual encounters, telephone conversation eg 'How do you do?', 'How are you?', 'Fine thanks', 'See you!', 'Well, must be getting on', 'It was nice to meet you'.

Discourse features

Discourse features means those structural or interactive features of talk (neither lexical nor grammatical) which reflect the nature of the exchange between speakers – how they relate to each other, how they express attentiveness, interest, attitude, emotion etc.

Listed below are some commonly used discourse features:

- use of discourse markers indicating interpersonal nature of exchanges eg tag questions, overlaps, interruptions, incomplete clauses

- repetitions and echoing between speakers eg 'She said she'd never speak to him again!' 'Never again? I can't believe she said never again'
- reformulation of utterances by speakers eg 'You mean that you have a problem, not that you'll never take a plane again. Be honest – say you have a problem with flying'
- back channel features (sometimes called monitoring devices or minimal responses). These are ways of indicating that a hearer is paying attention to the speaker eg sounds: 'mm', 'ah-ha', or short words: 'yeah', 'right', 'really', 'sure', 'yes', 'no'
- use of disjuncts (comments on style or truth/value of what is being said) eg 'frankly', 'honestly', 'confidentially'
- use of comment clauses (expressing speaker's feelings) eg *tentativeness*: 'I think', 'I suppose', 'they say'; *certainty*: 'I know', 'I'm sure', 'I must say', 'there's no doubt'; *emotional attitude*: 'I'm delighted to say', 'I'm afraid', 'Heaven knows', 'to be honest', 'frankly speaking', 'with all due respect'

ACTIVITY 18

Task: to identify selected discourse features in spontaneous interaction

Record a radio phone-in programme and note down all the occurrences of the following discourse features: tag questions, reformulations, back-channel features and comment clauses. You may want to listen to several similar programmes to get a wider view.

Fluency in talk

Fluency in talk (literally, 'flowing') is metaphoric, but has come to mean the ease by which spoken communication is managed. Even so, there is some ambiguity about easy communication – to call someone a smooth talker is no compliment! Fluency in talking might be represented as a *cline* or *continuum*, with almost complete fluency at one end of the cline, and virtual incoherence at the other. Most spoken interaction shows a balance between the two extremes, a kind of 'fluency norm', fluctuating according to who the speakers are and what they are talking about. Fluency is desirable to most of us and hence is the unmarked 'norm' of talking. Because non-fluency features deviate from this norm, they are marked. Listed below are some typical normal non-fluency features which can be found in most people's talking to a greater or lesser degree:

- hesitations – particularly those longer than a few seconds. Very frequent hesitations can have a serious effect on the listener, who may lose patience and stop attending
- false starts – this is when the speaker starts an utterance, then stops and either repeats it, or reformulates it: incomplete clauses (speaker trails off like this . . .)
- high proportion of fillers or other kinds of vague language like hedging devices
- repetitions – this is not a speech dysfunction (stuttering) but an over-frequent use of the same word or phrase

- excessive use of overlaps (when one speaker starts before another finishes)
- excessive use of interruptions (when a speaker starts to speak whilst another is talking)
- failure to identify and repair miscommunication
- failure to use such strategies as: clarification; shifting frames; adjusting schema; code-switching; conversational maxims and other politeness strategies in order to improve communication.

However, it should be noted that the degree of fluency in talking is not in itself evidence of success or failure within an interaction. We are all familiar with the stereotype of the smooth-talking villain and the stammering, hesitant hero (to be transformed into eloquence by the love of a good woman). Successful communication can take place with a substantial degree of non-fluency *if* the participants are comfortable with the situation, and if the language choices and the discourse strategies (conscious or unconscious) are all functioning effectively.

We are now in a position to recognise that effective communication is determined by many more complex factors than might have been assumed before. In the following chapters we shall apply some of the approaches to discourse analysis which have been outlined above, explore their lexical and grammatical realisations, and measure the levels of fluency, as we continue to investigate talk.

ACTIVITY 19

Task: to investigate levels of fluency in different contexts and with different participants

Choose *either* casual conversation *or* classroom interaction as a context for studying fluency in talk.

- **To study fluency levels in casual conversation**, select a number of occasions when friends or family are talking informally and try to identify the person who uses the most non-fluency features, and the person who uses the least. Take into account the influence of personality, situation, topic of conversation and other participants on their fluency levels. You may be able to construct a 'fluency profile' of each subject by noting the frequency and kind of non-fluency features used. Report back your findings to the group.
- **To study fluency levels in classroom interaction**, ask permission to record all or part of a teaching session, preferably without the class being aware of the recording. Select an extract to study in detail, and note down the kind of non-fluency features appearing in the exchanges between the participants. Tabulate your findings and present them to the group.

3 Talking in Private: Unplanned Speech

If you were to carry a dictaphone with you from the moment you got up till the moment you went to bed (and then left it switched on in case you talked in your sleep), you would accumulate a vast amount of fascinating data. It might include casual conversation with friends and family; formal or informal encounters with strangers in shops or on public transport; discussion with colleagues or fellow students; meetings, interviews or consultations with a range of different professionals; and even monologues when you were talking to yourself (a more frequent occurrence than you'd expect). The talking would be immensely varied, and would reveal your communicative competence as you made smooth transitions and changes both within and between different situations. An observer would note your confident capacity (derived from previous experience) and remarkable skill in accommodating your spoken language to all these different situations and people. An observer might also note that the way you spoke to friends and family was rather different from the way you talked to members of the public or colleagues at work. In the next three chapters we shall be using these differences between private talking and public talking as ways of structuring our investigation, in spite of the rather broad nature of the categories *public* and *private*. A further differentiation will be between planned and unplanned talk (most private informal talk is spontaneous, and much public talking is scripted).

What is meant by *unplanned private talking* is interaction in a context where the participants know each other well or reasonably well, and where the interaction is in some way personal, if not necessarily domestic. Unplanned or spontaneous interaction is more likely between intimate or familiar participants; in a private context we can expect a higher proportion of implicatures, more non-fluency features, more overlaps and interruptions. (There can be exceptions, however; talking in private may sometimes be planned if the speaker has something important to say, pleasant or unpleasant.)

What is meant by *unplanned public talking* is interaction in a context where the participants do not know each other well, and perhaps not at all. There is usually a strongly transactional function in the talking. Unplanned interaction in a public context tends to be associated with service encounters or professional consultations. There may still be many non-fluency features, but fewer overlaps, latched talk and interruptions. Again, there can be exceptions; talking in public in a non-personal context can lead to unplanned responses, if the speaker's expectations of the interview or consultation are not met. (*Planned public interaction* tends to be associated with occupational, business, professional, civic or national contexts, and is often learnt in advance, or even scripted.)

Nevertheless, despite the exceptions cited above, it remains broadly the case that the categories *private/public* and *unplanned/planned* are workable. In this chapter we shall look at private and unplanned talking, making full use of the theoretical and analytic frameworks described earlier, to investigate an extensive range of data, focusing on the most accessible (and often most complex) kind of talking in private – *casual conversation*. The data will be interactional, transactional, or both, depending on context and participants.

If we select from a single day all the instances of casual conversation we have participated in or listened to, the list of examples is likely to be long. Predominantly dialogic (with two or more participants), there might also be instances of monologic speech (thinking aloud, telling a joke or anecdote *within* a conversation, leaving answer-phone messages, talking to a voice-activated computer). Below, we shall investigate the following dialogic examples: informal conversation with family and friends; talking informally on the telephone; telling jokes and anecdotes; talking to different kinds of audiences (elderly people, animals, children, someone who is unwell); we shall also look briefly at a selection of answer-phone messages.

Casual conversation: family and friends

Transcript 6: talking at home
If you have a copy of the *Living Language Cassette,* you will find Transcript 6 on it as 'Investigating Talk Extract 2'.

S and R are female, D is S's boyfriend and C is R's boyfriend. All are 18–24 in age. M is the mother of S and R. The participants are chatting over tea

S	but it's sort of like sateeny material
C	sateen
S	you know what I mean don't you
M	well (4.0) like underskirt material
S	yes
R [ ]	S you didn't like your new new uniform and it's quite nice
S	no (.) I've just got too much style
C	well
M	has Dad finished talking over the garden wall
D	yeah I saw him putting the things away in the shed
S	what time's ...
M	or is it twenty to D (.) you'd better have a look 'cos I can't miss 5 minutes of it and there's only about three episodes to go

[*television programme being watched by M, S and D*]

R	would you like some more cheese and tomato
C	what about your dad (.)

R   Mum can make him some more (.) I can make you some more talking about making some more

C   I've got a little lump come up on my finger look

R   [*laughs*]

M   what have you been doing C—

C   what (.) I've got this thingy lump on my finger

R [ ]   it's the smallest thing the size of a pinhead

C [ ]   you don't know these things (.) could have my finger chopped off or something like that

R   we saw a rottweiler today

C   yeah a big lad wa'nt he

R [ ]   um enormous (3.0)

S   we saw loads of Great Danes didn't we (2.0) I think they're coming into fashion

M   and everyone was out with their new-born babies

S   oh I know

D   [*chokes on sandwich*]

M   oh D— do you want a drink of tea?

D   [*chokes*]

S   blossom have some tea

C   I think the cheese and pickle sandwiches were nice (.) D— was trying to get three in his mouth at once I think

D   (.) I thought if I had a drink of tea (.) sort of R— would have a faceful (.) thought I'd better hang on a second

M   yes everyone was out with their new-born babies and their dogs

(Source: Rosalind Preston)

COMMENTARY   In this extract we shall focus on a few specific features and suggest others to investigate further. Speaker shifts are frequent and often linked with topic shifts: for example, in the first section up to the television programme being turned on there are three topics – the material, Dad in the garden and the television programme. In the second section the topics are sandwiches, Dad's needs, the lump on C's finger, dogs and babies.

ACTIVITY 20

1   Note how different speakers introduce topics. Look at the frequency of vague language ('sort of like', 'you know what I mean', 'this thingy lump', 'something like that') and at the colloquial lexis ('a big lad wa'nt he', 'loads of Great Danes', 'a faceful', 'hang on a second') and terms of endearment ('blossom').

2   Look at the use of interrogatives, phatic language and non-fluency features.

Transcript 7: making a request

Husband J and wife M talking from respective studies

M   are you coming upstairs

J   is there something you want

M   could you bring me my diary it's by the phone

J   yes OK

(Source: Susan Cockcroft, 1999)

COMMENTARY   Note the conversational implicature: **M**'s question implies the following: if you are coming upstairs could you bring me something. **J**'s response shows that the implicature has been understood and asks for clarification. **M**'s response is to request the diary, followed by a statement of its location. **J** agrees to the request. This is a *transactional* exchange.

ACTIVITY 21

Look out for conversational implicatures in exchanges with family and close friends and note down two or three examples. Discuss your findings, and note frequency of usage. Is this linked with individual idiolects or context led?

Casual conversation: telling stories and jokes

Transcript 8

Transcript 8 is on the *Living Language Cassette* as 'Investigating Talk Extract 3'.

The participants are the same as in Transcript 6

R	was that Emma (4.0)
S	it was rea ... quite funny cause when we went to the pictures last night their car was actually parked behind ours (1.0) is that mine
D [ ]	tell us the whole story
S	what
D	what did you do
S	well I wrote a letter to them
D	no before that what did you take off one car and put on another
M	S—
S	ooh (.) oh yes
M	what have you been doing
S	ooh (.) you know if you park in that one place in the Eagle Centre
C	and they give you a
M	is that all right R—
S [ ]	yes and they give you one of those really sticky tickets
M [ ]	umm [ ] is it nice
C	yeah
S	well we peeled it off D—'s
D	I've said um I collect them and I've got millions of =
M [ ]	what did you peel off D—'s
D =	them on my car
S	a you shouldn't be parking here ticket
D	and as they've said um (.) you're parked in like a prohibited place (.) note has been taken of your registration (.)
C	if you do it again we
D [ ]	yeah we'll prosecute you (.) and I'd just cleaned my car (.) beautiful (.) and went for a pizza and we'd just got one of these labels stuck on (.) God (.) so we went to the UCI parked the car and we couldn't get in at that night so thought we'd come back at nine o'clock and I peeled (.) well between us (.) we peeled the sticker off and S— got it and stuffed it on the car next to us

C	didn't know who it was
D	no [*laughs*]
C	the bloke will be (.) the bloke will be wondering (.) humph (.) won't park in that spot again will I or something
D	(.) you can carry on from there it's your story
S	(.) and then [*mouth full*]
M	pardon
C	and then [*imitates S*]
S	we popped back so you could see against all odds and Tab and Sue were there (.) Tab's his brother
C	umm
M [ ]	when today
S	no last night
D [ ]	last night
S	and said (.) we're going to the pictures and they said (.) so are we (.) well we're going to see Sleeping with the Enemy (.) so are we (.) well we're going to the UCI (.) so are we but they didn't because they couldn't get in 'cos we got tickets early (.) so [*blows a raspberry*]
C	so it's still selling out then is it
S	yeah
C	umm
S	to be noted
C [ ]	we thought it wouldn't be
S	(.) anyway we parked the car and there was Tim's car behind us (.) which was quite shocking really out of all the cars that could have been at the back
M [ ]	well yes
S	so I stuck a note to their window screen
R [ ]	now look I know when you think a car is someone's you thought Bev and Mick's car was in a drive =
S [ ]	yes but this was
R =	in Findern or something =
S [ ]	yes
R =	and it wasn't theirs at all
S	I know but this really was theirs
D [ ]	got the registration
S	yes (.) and then when we got back there was a note stuck to ours saying yes we woz 'ere to
M	[*laughs*]
S	and that was it really (.) quite an extraordinary amount of coincidences (5.0)

(Source: Rosalind Preston)

COMMENTARY   This is a complex narrative in three stages:

- part 1 (up to **D**'s comment 'you can carry on from there it's your story')
- part 2 (up to **C** ''cos we thought it wouldn't be')
- part 3 to the end.

Labov's narrative structure theory (abstract, orientation, evaluation, narrative, result and coda) can be applied to the whole story (see p27). **S**'s statement 'it was rea ... quite funny ...' provides the *abstract* or summary; the *orientation* or context is the conversation about car park labels; the *evaluation* or point of interest is the fact that they didn't know whose car was parked next to them; the *narrative* is the account of what happened, including *complicating action* clauses such as the coincidence of seeing friends at the cinema and the difficulty of getting cinema tickets. The *result* is that the note 'we woz 'ere' was left on their car, and the *coda* or ending is **S**'s remark 'quite an extraordinary amount of coincidences'.

ACTIVITY 22

1 Look at **S** and **D**'s use of collaborative narrative strategies (it is not a monologic anecdote); opening and closing framing devices; the use of back-channel and monitoring responses as well as comments on the action by the audience.

2 Record two friends or family members telling a story together and compare the strategies used with this transcript.

Transcript 9: extract from personal narrative (monologue)

*The monologue is part of a naval officer's (**P**'s) account of being in a tropical storm in Singapore when his ship was anchored in a crowded harbour, and the safest option was to get to sea as fast as possible to ride out the storm (Transcription edited and simplified)*

P   I suppose (.) I fell asleep and the story begins with (.) I was (.) seemed to be getting buffeted about and pushed and kicked and as I opened my eyes (.) I (.) now as I look back I can remember seeing an almost crazy scene of stars swinging about above my head you see (.) I now know of course that I was looking through the skylight and it was literally (.) it wasn't the stars that were swinging about (.) but the ship was being heaved this way and that and there was (.) I could alreadysense commotion and excitement . . .
[*he hurried on deck, realised that his ship, being moored to a much larger one, was in danger of being smashed into its side*]
(.) at one minute the ship would go down and there would be a sort of wanton sag in the ropes and the (.) another minute it would be thrown taut 'n like (.) sort of (.) a terrier (.) a mad terrier on a leash or something tugging like this you see
[*people on deck were letting go the ropes as he hurried to the bridge, frantically ringing down to start the engines as they began to drift towards a very large Dutch merchant ship*]
well (.) it (.) it's a hideous feeling to be completely incapable of doing anything when you know you're going to have a first class collision (.) account for it to (.) with a court martial and all this you see (.) all this I can now tell you with some (.) not exactly mirth in retrospect but at least (.) you know (.) I've told the experience so (.) I (.) I (.) see it differently from the panic that I (.) well I hope I wouldn't (4.0) panic (5.0) on the deck of this Dutchman they were bawling you know as if I didn't know you see (6.0) I was frantically trying to get (.) going (.) well at the very very last few feet (.) I mean one tends to say the last second (.) the last moment and this (.) but I know there was a few feet in it (.) suddenly the engines burst into life

(Source: data provided courtesy of Christine Fletcher)

COMMENTARY

The narrator is re-living a traumatic experience, and it is not surprising that there are numerous false starts (eg 'story begins with' . . . 'I was' . . . 'seemed to be'). Although this is a continuous monologue there is an audience, indicated by the interactional features like 'you see', 'I can now tell you'.

1 Identify Labov's stages of narrative in this monologic anecdote. Your focus will be on the use of framing devices, interactional features and non-fluency features.
2 Look for examples of vague language and incomplete utterances. Why do you think they appear in this kind of narrative?

3 Initiate and record a different kind of narrative with friends: a joke-telling session. Working in pairs, identify and compare the use of narrative structure in each joke.

Casual conversation: talking on the telephone

Three transcripts of telephone conversations follow: the commentary will be found at the end of Transcript 12.

Transcript 10: talking with a college friend

If you have a copy of the *Living Language Cassette*, you will find Transcript 10 on it as 'Investigating Talk Extract 4'.

I and S are A-Level students (male)

S	I—
I	yes
S	hello
I	what did you do in English
S	we didn't do anything really
I	did you do your projects
S	no because he was away
I	was he
S	yes
I	that was fortunate

[*passage omitted*]

S	have you been doing your project today at home
I	well I recorded the fight on Saturday and I've just done the transcripts today (.) and then I've got to type them up on my computer
S	right
I	there's no point in me doing anything in the lesson anyway (.) because it's all on the computer I've got to do it
S	yes (.) so you're not going to go in tomorrow then
I	well I probably will (.) because I've got to go to geography anyway
S	yes see I've got loads of things to ask him
I	have you got any other lessons in the afternoon anyway
S	er economics
I	yes so might as well go and see if he's there
S	right (.) I've just rang P— (.) about my economics homework
I	did he sound really nervous
S	he's always nervous isn't he really
I	I think he sounds really nice on the phone
S	yes (.) he's (.) a nice boy

I	he's lovely (.) OK see you [*I imitates P*] see you tomorrow
S	all nervous (.) er
I [ ]	a bit like you actually
S	I'm not nervous on the phone
I	you are
S	why
I	you sound nervous
S	do I
I	yes
S	I'm sorry
I	oh

[*passage omitted*]

I	well it was lovely speaking to you
S	no it wasn't (.) don't lie
I	well actually it was very boring
S	thanks a lot
I	no it was lovely
S	no be honest
I	I can't
S	OK (.) er (.) I'm going (.) 'cos I've got loads of homework to do (.) and it's now =
I =	yes but (.) will you actually do any of it
S	er (.) it's twenty-five to eight and I always say I'll start on the hour
I	right
S	because my clock chimes you see (.) but then I never do
I	OK
S	you see (.) so I probably won't
I	I know what you're talking about
S	OK
I	even if the rest of the world doesn't
S	OK (.) I knew you'd understand
I	OK (.) see you tomorrow
S	OK then
I	bye
S	b-bye

(Source: Stephen Jephson)

Transcript 11: talking with a close friend

If you have a copy of the *Living Language Cassette*, you will find Transcript 11 on it as 'Investigating Talk Extract 5'.

S and H are male (aged 17–18) and good friends

H	hello
S	hello is that H
H	yes
S	it's S
H	oh (.) all right
S	how are you
H	I'm OK (.) thanks very much [*stupid voice*]
S	good lad (.) have you seen the paper (.) the *Burton Mail*
H	no
S	er (.) well you're in it
H	am I

S	yes
H	what
S	well (.) you know you played well (.) didn't you
H	yes
S	well hey (.) you played brilliantly
H	yes
S	well you're in the *Burton Mail*
H	am I
S	yes (.) player of the match and all this lot
H	really (.) well what's it say
S	man of the match and it says (.) H laid all the goals up (.) and this lot (.) so I'll bring it round to you now (.) if you want
H	yes (.) I wouldn't mind (.) ta
S	because I'm coming past
H	ah (.) cheers mate (.) are you going out tonight
S	there's supposed to be a party at Vines (.) isn't there
H	yes I'm going with A— I think
S	are you going
H	yes
S	good lad (.) and when you going (.) what time
H	well I'm gonna have me tea (.) then I was going to walk down to A—'s
S	OK (.) I'll be round in a bit
H	OK (.) see you in a bit then
S	OK see you
H	cheers

(Source: Stephen Jephson)

Transcript 12: elderly mother talking to her daughter

If you have a copy of the *Living Language Cassette*, you will find Transcript 12 on it as 'Investigating Talk Extract 6'.

V is the mother of J, and a grandmother. They are discussing what to do with a surplus cooker and how J's father-in-law is settling into a residential home.

V	because they have them for people who want stuff (.) you know (.) people who are really desperate for stuff
J	I had thought of that actually (.) because there's the cooker (.) if we can't get rid of the cooker (.) might do that (.) because that's spotless that is
V	is it
J	yes (.) an electric one
V	oh (.) dear
J	well the oven was never used mum
V	no
J	just a shame nobody could do with it (.) erm you know so (.)
V	yes (.) bugger i'nt it
J	it's really (.) anyway (.) just wanted to get everything out (.)
V	how's C's dad anyway
J	settling in (.) I think he's ruling the roost in there (.) ordering people about
V	oh ah
J	he seems to have settled in (.) that social services man said if he's not right (.) we'll make sure he does but (.) you can't vet everybody can you
V	she says (.) I will get you one soon (.) so he says (.) I keep coming up here and asking you (.) so she said look (.) there's really (.) really (.) sick people in here (.) besides you

J	anyway (.) I'll go and do some ironing now (.) never ending (.) yes put your legs up (.) take care of yourself (.) give us a ring if you want anything
V	OK then J
J	b-bye then mum
V	yes (.) bye-bye

(Source: Stephen Jephson)

COMMENTARY In each of the telephone conversations, greetings, opening and closing moves can be identified ('hello, hello is that H', 'OK see you tomorrow', 'OK then', 'bye', 'b-bye', 'OK see you in a bit then', 'OK see you', 'cheers', 'OK then J', 'b-bye then mum', 'yes bye-bye').

ACTIVITY 24

1 Note and find examples of the differing length of turns, and the frequency of adjacency pairs in Transcript 10. Is there any linguistic evidence that the speakers in Transcript 11 are closer friends than those in Transcript 10? What effect does gender have on these three exchanges?

2 With the agreement of the telephone user, record an agreed period of telephone conversations (one way). Identify the differences between the speaker's responses to different callers, noting particularly the use of phatic language, opening and closing moves, topic shifts and back-channel behaviour.

Casual conversation: talking to different audiences

We know that people talk differently to babies and young children (motherese, fatherese, parentese, baby talk or caretaker language) than they do to older children and adults. This difference in language seems to be associated with an inequality in the relationship between the adult who has *power* and the child who is relatively *powerless*.

The same language differences can occur in comparable personal relationships between, for example, pet owners and their animals, or those caring for the elderly or sick, and seems to imply a linguistically inadequate audience, or pseudo-audience, as David Crystal describes the infant.

Characteristic features of caretaker language include basic turn-taking, a tendency to simplify structures, shorten utterances, exaggerate intonation and pitch patterns, use diminutive or re-duplicated forms, and to correct non-grammatical usage, mispronunciation or lexical errors.

Talking to children

Transcript 13: talking to a very young child
Mother M talks to A aged 3 months

A	[smiles]
M	oh what a nice little smile (.) yes (.) isn't that nice (.) there (.) there's a nice little smile
A	[burps]
M	what a nice little wind as well (.) yes that's better isn't it (.) yes (.)
A	[vocalises]
M	there's a nice little noise …
M	… [removes A's bottle] are you finished (.) yes (.) well (.) was that nice

Mother M talks to A age 18 months

A	[blowing noises]
M	that's a bit rude
A	mouth
M	mouth (.) that's right
A	face
M	face (.) yes (.) mouth is in your face (.) what else have you got in your face
A	face [closing eyes]
M	you're making a face aren't you

(Source: Snow, 1977, cited in McTear, 1985)

Transcript 14: talking to a three year old child
Researcher R talking to L (aged 3). Both participants are female

R	right then what are you going to draw
L	erm (.) they're Christopher's
R	pardon
L	they're Christopher's
R	yeah they're Christopher's crayons (.) whose are those
L	they're Jon's
R	and whose are those
L	(.) those (.) are yours these are Chris's
R	yep (.) so what are you going to draw then
L	I'm gonna draw (1) a lovely lovely ha- lovely lo- ha- house
R	a house
L	yeah
R	can I draw one as well
L	yeah (.) I can't draw a house (.) let me do (.) a triangle (1) there's a triangle
R	that's not a triangle (1.0) that's a triangle isn't it
L	um (.) I can't do that shall we co-colour that up
R	yeah if you want
L	[*colours in picture*] there we are

(Source: Ann Henderson)

ACTIVITY 25

1 Look for use of repetition and simplified and short utterances.

2 If you have the *Living Language Cassette*, listen to Extract 1 and identify the examples of exaggerated intonation patterns.

COMMENTARY In the three transcripts a gradual change can be seen in the language of the adult speaking to the child; the mother talking to A at 3 months treats any noise or change of expression as if it were a turn, and she also invents a response and conducts a dialogue with herself ('oh what a nice little smile … yes … isn't that nice … there'); in the second exchange she reformulates and expands the child's words ('face … yes mouth is in your face'). In Transcript 14 the adjacency pairs structure is clearly established.

Talking to animals

As we have noted, many people talk to domestic pets as if they were young children. The same exaggerated intonation patterns, the same shortening of utterances, the same tendency to use baby-talk can be observed. Domestic animals recognise turn-taking and learn to respond to human words, though people who work with animals professionally (farmers, equestrians, zoo and circus staff) have a more pragmatic and less emotional relationship with their animals.

Transcript 15
*Owner **M** talking to cat **Z** while feeding it*

M	Z—
Z	meow
M	Z—
Z	meow meow
M	now what do you want (.) come on then (.) come on Z—Z [*diminutive form*] (.) let's go downstairs (.) come on then (.) come on then (.) come on
Z	wow wow wow (.) prrumph
M	do you want some tea then (.)
Z	prrumph
M	Z— (.) yes (.) come on then
Z [ ]	wow

[*pause whilst food is being prepared, cat climbs on kitchen table*]

M	[*places cat's food on floor*] here you are then baby (.) here you are (.) here

[*cat looks anxiously up from food*]

M	come on Z— it's OK (.) gosh (.) you were a hungry boy then weren't you

[*cat finishes eating, moves towards back door*]

M	do you want to go out

[*cat exits without response; minutes later M meets cat by garden door*]

M	hello chicken (.) what you're doing (.) do you want to go out (.)
Z	meeeow

(Source: Susan Cockcroft, 1999)

COMMENTARY The owner elicits vocalised responses from the cat in a turn-taking sequence until the food is presented. After this the cat makes no further response apart from the final turn. Note the owner's use of terms of endearment and repetition.

Talking to the elderly

We might expect that talking to old people would be the same as talking to other adults, but this is often not the case. Some people assume that the elderly are in their second childhood and address them in caretaker language. This can cause distress or annoyance to people, who feel patronised by their carers, whether medical or support staff. Even in the family an old person may be spoken to in this way. Exaggerated intonation patterns, shortened utterances, simplified syntax, even 'baby names' may be used by well-meaning carers. The elderly person may be talked about as if not present or capable of making his own decisions, eg 'Daddy wants some soup, don't you, Daddy'; or the third person form may be used, assuming him unable to respond 'Does he want some soup?' Similar linguistic patronising can affect other disempowered groups – people who are ill, and people with long- or short-term special needs, whether physical, mental, emotional or psychological. Indeed, feeling vulnerable (for whatever reason) makes most of us want to be looked after like a child (at least temporarily). We accept people speaking in simple, uncomplicated and reassuring language, when we feel ill or frightened, and even some degree of exaggerated intonation patterns. For people with long-term or permanent disability the assumptions are that disability means incapacity, and that caretaker language is required. Below is an example of an elderly person who refuses to be patronised.

Transcript 16
*These extracts are taken from an interview which took place in the 1950s between **Mr C**, a 103-year-old resident of Tunbridge Wells, and **I**, a female interviewer*

I	well now Mr C (.) you tell me (.) about Tunbridge We . . lls=
Mr C =	I don't know anything about … Tunbridge Wells
I	but you've lived here (.) I believe (.) since you were 18=
Mr C =	that's right
I	and has it changed much in all that time
Mr C	yes (.) we had a lotta changes
I	what's what's the biggest change do you think
Mr C [ ]	well er (.) lotta building an (1.5) 's all I know about it (.) about Tunbridge Wells (0.5)
I	What's the nicest thing about Tunbridge Wells =
Mr C =	what's what
I	what's the nicest thing (.) about Tunbridge Wells
Mr C [ ]	I don't know
I	don't you know anything nice about it
Mr C	no
I	nothing at all
Mr C	no I know nothing about Tunbridge Wells
I	but it must be a healthy place
Mr C	mm
I	it must be a healthy place =
Mr C =	oh it's a healthy place cos you can go back (.) to the fif- (.) fifteenth and sixteenth century can't you (1.0)

I	yes (.) I know any
Mr C [ ]	bet you don't know that (0.5)
I	oh yes (.) I knew that (.) but any ways
Mr C [ ]	oh
I	it must be healthy (.) for you to be (.) looking so wonderful (.) at this age
Mr C	well why shouldn't I look wonderful (1.0)
I	mm (.) well erm that of course comes from the inner spirit I know
Mr C	mm
I	that comes from the inner spirit (1.0)
Mr C	mm
I [ ]	well from your own inner spirit
Mr C	(2.5) I don't know what you want me to say (.) if I can say anything to please you I will but
I [ ]	what you're saying delights me (.) I
Mr C [ ]	mm
I	want you to tell me something about living in Tunbridge Wells

[*passage omitted*]

I	erm and (.) can you tell me anything (.) about changes in transport there (.) I suppose once upon a time there were horses where now there are motorcars
Mr C	no I can't tell you anything about that (0.5)
I	you don't remember that
Mr C	well I dare say I could remember but I didn't have any business in it (.) that's the thing makes you remember when you got some money in it

[*passage omitted*]

I	Just to finish off would you tell us your full name (.) and how old you are now
Mr C	true name my name
I [ ]	your full name
Mr C	my full name (.) Alfred Cranwell (1.5)
I	and how old are you (1.0)
Mr C	born in eighteen fifty one (.) first o'January and you can work that out for yourself can't you

(Source: cited in Langford, 1994)

Transcript 17

*A young woman **Y** is talking to an elderly woman **E** about her mother's house being burgled*

Y	and that's made her nervous you know I think once something like that
E [ ]	yes (.) of course (.) how old is she
Y	she's seventy two
E	I'm seventy eight
Y	[*astonished*] are you
E	yes
Y	[*gasps*] gosh you're marvellous aren't you
E	[*laughing slightly*] I don't know
Y	oh gosh you are I'd never have thought (.) you've got lovely skin [*touches cheeks, laughs*] you have haven't you
E	[*touches cheeks, laughs*] oh I don't know [*laughs*]
Y	[*emphatically*] oh you have =
E =	yeah
Y	my mother (.) looks the same sort as you
E [ ]	does she

Y [ ]   she she looks
E [ ]   yes yes
Y   younger than her age and she's got a great outlook on life

(Source: cited in Coupland, 1991)

COMMENTARY The two transcripts show quite different ways of talking to old people. Transcript 16 shows the interviewer being stalled at every point in the interview by her combative subject ('why shouldn't I look wonderful'), who constantly tries to wrong-foot her ('bet you don't know that'). The participants in Transcript 17 are talking co-operatively.

ACTIVITY 26

Discuss what has gone wrong in the first interview and right in the second. You may find it helpful to look at opening and closing moves, the kind of questions being asked, lexical choice, use of tag questions, phatic language, and non-fluency features.

Talking as monologue

The book so far has focused primarily on the dialogic nature of spoken language. But monologue is also part of our earliest experience of speech. Young children frequently accompany their actions with a running commentary ('Teddy in bath get soap water hot Teddy don't cry Teddy go bed now night night sleep tight'). The child is his or her own audience. In adult spoken language, monologue tends to be reported negatively by the listener ('it was nothing but an endless *monologue* – he went on and on … it drove me mad'). Planned monologue in literary or dramatic contexts is, however, entirely acceptable (eg Alan Bennett's *Talking Heads* or Shakespeare's soliloquies).

Probably the most frequent use of monologue by adults is when we are thinking aloud: this could be to remind ourselves ('now I mustn't forget to include this in Chapter 4'); or to deal with a practical problem ('should I borrow a copper-bottomed pan or will the ordinary saucepan do – I'm late already'); or to present a complex argument in an exam answer ('if capitalism is becoming an outdated theory, is Marxist economic theory a better option, or should we …').

More recently we are often required to leave a monologic message on an answering machine, addressing an absent audience, with no idea when our message will be answered (if at all).

If the response comes when we are absent and our answering machine is switched on, it can lead to a drawn out dialogue in slow motion, achieved through an exchange of monologic messages! Emotions can be involved in this context: when people telephone and an answering machine responds, reactions vary. Some people hang up immediately! Most people manage to leave a short, reasonably business-like message, but others stumble and hesitate, apparently losing confidence in their capacity to talk to an absent audience, and leaving garbled messages. Others speak with confidence and at length, as if actually engaged in dialogue with the absent audience, even making their message interactional rather than transactional. The data below provides a range of monologic answer-phone language.

Transcript 18

The following sequences have been taken from a private answering machine: only personal messages have been transcribed

Message 1 (male, middle aged)
M (.) it's P ringing from H. .(.) [*gives number*] I'm ringing on Friday the eighteenth (.) and erm sorry not Friday the eighteenth whatever it is sorry I've got er (.) a re-entry problem after Italy you must bear in mind [*laughs*] (.) it takes a little time to get sorted out (.) but I'm not going to take up time on your answer-phone except to say that I'm actually ringing on Friday the twenty eighth of August [*coughs loudly*] do you hear (.) I've got a terrible cold as a result of the climatic change (.) erm it's simply to say that T and I would like to have a word with you erm (.) when you get back (.) and erm T's hoping to see you on the nineteenth and twentieth of September if possible (.) or thereabouts when I'm in Italy for a conference ... but er we've got lots of other things to talk about (.) so (.) look forward to being in touch with (.) you hope things have gone well for you and you've had a good time (.) and erm we'll hear from you soon (.) bye for now

Message 2 (female, mid-twenties)
Hello (.) it's P here (.) have you got my post card from Spain (.) I haven't spoken to both of you for ages I'm in tonight so give me a ring if you're around (.) otherwise give me a ring sometime over the weekend I'd love to speak to you both (.) OK then byee

Message 3 (female, middle aged)
I think you must be away because your phone's running out (.) only M to see if you're all right and there are beds free here now (.) bye

Message 4 (female, middle aged)
Hello this is AP (.) happy bank holiday (.) this is to say I'm sorry I can't get to the magazine meeting this week (.) we're going to a funeral and I don't think we'll be back in time (.) it's down in London (.) thank you

Message 5 (male, mid-twenties)
I see you've got lots of messages (.) so I'll keep this brief (.) it's just K ringing up to wish N a happy birthday (.) well happy birthday N erm (.) I'll see you all soon (.) goodbye

(Source: Susan Cockcroft, 1999)

COMMENTARY   The messages are all personal; the callers are male and female, and the age range is from mid-twenties to middle age. All the messages are apparently transactional, although Message 4 has some interactional function and may involve a conversational implicature ('please get in touch').

ACTIVITY 27

Note and list examples of opening and closing moves, incomplete utterances and non-fluency features. You may wish to consider the possible effects of gender, age and personality on the language choices in each message.

4 Talking in Public: Unplanned Speech

Talking in public is what we do all the time when we're not talking in private! In other words, this includes all the spoken interactions that are part of our everyday life as we go to work, catch a bus or train, shop, visit the bank, buy a stamp or a newspaper, choose a new outfit, attend a class or consult a doctor or lawyer. Public talk is predominantly transactional, though there may also be interactional elements providing necessary 'social lubrication'. Participants in public talk may know each other as friends or acquaintances or they may be complete strangers. What matters is that in a particular situation, the talking takes place not in the domestic and private context, but in the worlds of education, business, media or other professional contexts, where a wider ranging public audience is addressed.

What our examples of talking in public also have in common is that the language used is relatively *unplanned* or spontaneous. This does not mean that there are no recognisable or predictable structures. Most transactional exchanges have characteristic structural patterns, depending on the situation, which participants recognise and follow, though flexibility and variation in idiolect and register are retained. If we define such exchanges as genres, it is possible to say that each genre has its own unique generic structure.

In this chapter we shall be investigating a range of differing spoken genres, all of which have characteristic structural features. Indeed, we know what to expect in our public talking, whether it takes place in the classroom, at the doctor's, in the local shop or listening to a radio phone-in and if our expectations are not met, the exchange has been unsuccessful. Expectations are based on what we remember of the genre from previous experience (*frame and schema theory*) and on our recognition of its patterning or structure (*generic structure potential*).

The data selected here includes a range of different unplanned (or partially planned) public talk: service encounters (business and professional); classroom interaction; court-room language; media talk including chat-shows, radio phone-ins, sports commentary; public information language (eg air traffic control). We can expect much variation in lexical choice, but more consistency in structural features.

Service encounters: business and professional

The term *service encounters* has been used to describe a wide range of transactional talking. Ruqaiya Hasan (1978) defines service encounters as requests for a service made by one person to another (eg visiting the doctor, shopping in the market). Eija Ventola (1987) developed this definition further in her study of service encounters at a post office, a travel agency and a gift shop. Following Hasan's generic structure theory (every genre has its unique structural pattern or GSP [*generic structure potential*]), Ventola identified a structural pattern common to all these service encounters:

- an offer of service
- a request for service
- a transaction
- a salutation.

Ventola's evidence supports Hasan's generic structure potential theory. Put simply, we know what form or structure to expect in any genre (anything from fairy stories and jokes to newspaper articles and visiting the doctor) because of our previous experience (see the discussion of frame and schema theory in Chapter 2). Hasan argues that every genre will have *obligatory* and *optional* elements. In the structural pattern described above, Ventola identifies the obligatory elements of service encounters. Further optional elements may be seen in the data below, which includes shop and market stall transactions, door-to-door canvassing, as well as doctor-patient consultation. Moreover, the GSP theory can be fruitfully applied to other genres in this chapter as well as to the genres (public and planned) discussed in Chapter 5.

Service encounters: business

Transcript 19: service message (goods) via answer phone
The speaker is an art restorer

Hello this is DH erm (.) I'm just ringing to let you know that (.) the work on the watercolour is now completed (.) so if you'd like to give me a ring (.) to arrange a collection time (.) thanks very much (.) bye bye

(Source: Susan Cockcroft, 1999)

COMMENTARY The service of restoring the watercolour has already been requested and the task is complete. The restorer requests the completion of the transaction (ie collection of picture and payment). Because this is a monologic message, the encounter remains incomplete, but the conversation implicature is that a response should be forthcoming from the initiator of the transaction. Note the framing devices and interactional language.

Transcript 20: service encounter in shop (goods)

S is the sales person, C the customer

C   excuse me young man (2.0) I'm looking for a bag for me shopping (2.0) have you got any

S   yeah erm the shopping bags are over there behind that stand

C   here

S   yeah see them

C   oh yeah (5.0) these are all right how much are they

S   they're four fifty but these (3.0) these are only erm three ninety nine

C   they're nice (3.0) only three ninety nine that's good that is isn't it

S   yeah we sell a lot of them (1.0) very good bags

C   I don't know which to have now (.) erm (3.0) oh I'll take that one

S   what blue

C   yeah that'll do (.) three ninety nine did you say

S   yes please

C   OK (.) there you go

S   thank you (3.0) that's four that's five and here's your receipt

C   thanks

S   thank you

(Source: James Hurdis)

Transcript 21: service encounter in shop (goods)

Participants as above

C   hello

S   hello

C   I'm looking for a leather handbag

S   well we've got all these here behind me erm (4.0) what colour was it you were looking for

C   navy was what I really wanted

S   well there's all these down this end so what size about did you have in mind

C   I'm not sure really (.) what I think is erm (.) I've just got to see one I like really

S   OK why don't you come round here and then you might be able to see better

C   [*to husband*] here look after this will you

H   mmm (4.0)

C   something like this (.) this one's nice do you like this one

H   yeah yeah it's OK

C   how much is this one

S   let's have a look (.) erm that one's twenty four ninety nine

C   that much

S   yeah it's Tula (.) they're a good quality bag

C   yes I know I've had one before (.) they are very good

H   have it if it's what yer want

C   oh I don't know (.) have you got anything a bit cheaper

S   yeah this one (.) it's only sixteen this one

C   no I don't know

H   if you want it have it

C   oh (.) oh go on then are you sure

H   yes

C   I'll have that one then please love

S   OK that's twenty four ninety nine then please (5.0) thank you there you go there's your penny and keep your (.) this (4.0) thanks

C   thank you bye

S   bye then

(Source: James Hurdis)

COMMENTARY These service encounters differ in length and complexity, but each follows Ventola's structural pattern (offer of service, request for service, transaction and salutation).

ACTIVITY 28

Identify these obligatory features in each transcript. Note the optional elements in Transcript 20 where **C** is given more information, leading to a delay in her decision. In Transcript 21 **C** and **S** have an extended exchange about the range of goods on offer; she also initiates an exchange with her husband before achieving the transaction. Note the frequency of adjacency pairs. Look too at politeness strategies, use of deictics and greetings.

Transcript 22: service encounter market stall (goods)

*The service encounter takes place in an outdoor market. **S** is the market stall assistant, **C** is the customer*

S   can I help you at all (.) or are you just looking
C   ner am just lookin thanks
S   all right (.) just give us a shout if yer want any help then

(Source: James Hurdis)

Transcript 23: service encounter market stall (goods)

Participants as above

S   are you all right
C   (.) er yeah could you give me some of the prices for the cases please
S   yeah which ones are you looking at in particular
C   well anything really (.) as long as it's got wheels on
S   erm they start with these (.) these are the cheapest
C   and how much are they
S   well it depends (3.0) I mean what size were you after
C   the ones we've got now are big ones
S   what thirty two inches
C   yeah that's right (4.0) and we'll be wanting (.) say erm one of them and perhaps a small 'un as well (3.0) so how much would these ones be
S   well (.) a thirty two in this is let's see erm (3.0) twenty eight ninety nine (3.0) and a what twenty four
C   yeah that's about right d'ya think love
Wife yeah
S   the twenty four is eighteen ninety nine (.) so together you're looking at nearly forty eight pounds altogether
C   OK then thanks for your help (3.0) we'll leave it for now (.) have a walk around and think about it
S   all right then bye

(Source: James Hurdis)

COMMENTARY All three market stall transcripts include the obligatory structural features; there are also some interesting differences between the two groups of transcripts (shop and market stall). Look particularly at lexis, terms of address, levels of formality, non-fluency features, and adjacency pairs. You may find the gender of the customers worth investigating.

Transcript 24: service encounter (door-to-door)

*S, a young male (aged 18) is trying to persuade a middle-aged female householder **T** to have a free damp survey done. His interview follows company guidelines (given below and not unlike Ventola's 'obligatory structural elements)*

- *say hello and apologise for disturbing them*
- *explain who you are working for – have they seen company's advertisements?*
- *describe process of damp survey and time taken*
- *ask if householder in on following day*
- *if yes make appointment, take name, address, telephone number, thank them and say goodbye*
- *if no explain that you are seeing many people in area, that survey is free, only takes minutes*
- *if they insist they don't want survey, leave them leaflet and say goodbye.*

S	hello there
T	hello
S	sorry to disturb you (.) don't worry I'm not trying to sell you any more windows [*laughs*]
T	no [*laughs*]
S	just from the Damp Detectors in D—
T	oh yes
S	probably seen our adverts in the local papers
T	well I have hmm
S	yeah (.) just in the area offering a free survey (.) a little electronic device run it across your wall and if we find any damp we advise you the best ways to get rid of it
T	yea
S	takes five to ten minutes at the most
T	oh when can you come
S	erm (.) ooh (.) what time's best for you tomorrow (.) are you in in the morning at all
T	oh no I've got to go out tomorrow (.) tomorrow aftern ... If I'll be in tomorrow afternoon it won't be er ... I'm not under any obligation or nothing
S	oh no (.) nothing like that
T	are you sure
S	yep (.) I'm absolutely positive about that (.) see (.) we're not just trying to con you into anything

[*passage omitted*]

S	apart from having the damp proofing course done
T	yes
S	and you know just to get rid of the damp and stop it appearing in other places
T	I (.) don't think I'm awful but I've got me stove on
S	oh right erm
T	I'm cooking me dinner
S	right err (.) is it Mr and Mrs or is it just yourself
T	no I'm on me own love
S	right (.) and it's (.) it's Mrs ...
T [ ]	T—

[*passage omitted*]

T	and I shouldn't be upset or anything
S	ah no (.) no
T	we've been talk like ... (.) only I shall have to talk it over with my sons tonight

S	yea
T	they both come tonight
S	like I say you're under no obligation
T	no
S	all he does is look round the exterior bricks
T [ ]	yea
S	I mean it's a waste of time taste ... tet ... testing there
T	yea
S	you know because they'd be moist even after a day like this
T	hmm
S	so what we do inside just above your skirting board (.) a proper damp course
T	do you have to come inside me duck
S	yea
T	yea
S	measure it ... I mean (.) they take it along there (.) if we find any damp you'll hear the
T [ ]	I shouldn't be upset or anything or hurt or anything
S	oh no no oh no no no nothing will be
T [ ]	no no no
S	hurt or destroyed or
T [ ]	well anyway (.) if I talk it over with my sons tonight and you come tomorrow afternoon (.) when are you coming
S	well what time's best for you
T	well

[*passage omitted*]

S	Wednesday (.) I'll just write it on there for ya (.) say we'll give you a ring before we pop round I would have thought it would be about two-ish
T	yes yes OK (.) and then yes as long as I'm not under any obligation
S	oh no no (.) nothing like that (.) I say all we do is give ya ... advise ya of five or six ways to get rid of it
T	yes OK
S	only takes ten minutes
T	yes OK
S	all right then (.) is there any more questions you'd like to ask me while I'm here
T	no I don't think so

[*passage omitted*]

S	yeah (.) we'll give you a ring just before we pop round
T	before you pop round (.) right
S	yeah all right then (.) thanks a lot then for your time then Mrs T—
T	shut me gate
S	yep (.) all right then (.) thanks a lot then
T	tada
S	see ya

(Source: Neil Wright)

Transcript 25: service encounter (door-to-door)

*The participants in this encounter are **S** (as above) and **B**, a male householder (aged 80)*

S	hello there (.) sorry to disturb you (.) don't worry I'm not trying to sell you any more windows or nothing (.) from Damp Detectors in D— (.) just in the area offering a free survey (.) would you be interested at all
B	brother I'm blind (.) I'm eighty years of age (.) does that answer ya
S	yeah I guess that means ya not bothered about it (.) all right then (.) thanks a lot anyway

> **B** bye
> **S** cheers

(Source: Neil Wright)

These two door-to-door encounters differ dramatically in length, although the basic structure is the same.

1 Identify the obligatory elements in each encounter; in Transcript 24 look for repetitions of structural patterns as well as repeated ideas.

2 Compare the way in which **S** addresses **T** with the way he addresses **B**. Look for use of terms of address, phatic language, non-fluency features and adjacency pairs.

Service encounters: professional

Although doctor-patient interviews are mainly transactional in nature, they do seem to differ from purchasing procedures, in that exchanges are likely to contain strong interactional elements. As non-experts in medical science, we ask the doctor's advice on a particular health problem. There is an immediate imbalance of power, which the well-trained doctor needs to address in order to make the patient feel as comfortable and equal as possible during the consultation. It can be done by choice of lexis, adjusting the level of medical jargon to the perceived preferences of patients; by adjusting register, framing devices and schema as appropriate; and by using interactional language within the transaction. The overall result should be a relaxed patient able to give full details of the problem so that an accurate diagnosis can be made.

In the diagnostic interview, the doctor must follow a specific set of procedures leading to particular outcomes: history-taking, physical examination, diagnosis and management. In taking a medical history the exchange structure model (see Chapter 2 (Coulthard and Brazil) involving two- or three-part exchanges) is most likely; physical examination may involve adjacency pairs and be non-verbal; the diagnosis will be doctor-centred initially (declaratives) though the patient may then initiate questions. The management stage will also be doctor-centred, with further questions or statements from the patient quite likely. The success of the consultation depends on the expectations of doctor and patient being met.

Such exchanges, together with similar professional consultations (counsellor-client, financial advisor-client, spiritual counsellor-client, lawyer-client), can be seen as specialised service encounters, requiring skilful management of the interactional with the transactional elements.

Transcript 26: service encounter: doctor-patient interview
P (female) is telling the doctor (D) about an injury to her back at work

P   yesterday I got home from work and [*inaudible*] the trouble is I can't bend forward and I can't turn sideways it's like the bottom of my spine it just feels like I'm sitting on a pin

D   so it's pain in the lower back

P   lower back just about there

D   OK how long did you say again

P   I mean all last night I couldn't turn on my side I couldn't stand up I couldn't go to the toilet

D   so it got worse overnight

P   yeh when I walk it hurts me to walk (.) I don't know what it I don't know if probably it's lifting the residents in the nursing home or what

D   no remembered injury (.) you don't remember doing anything in particular

P   I've worked with elderly people for ten years moving them around

D   waterworks OK

P   yeh fine

D   can you climb on the couch while I have a look at your back just lie flat on your back

P   lie back oh ooh [*inaudible*]

D   I'll give you a hand (.) just relax as best as you can (.) sorry (.) as you are comfortable OK

P   yeh

D   it's when you move

P   it's when I move and when I lie in bed back in the house I can't lie straight I have to lift my bottom up otherwise I can feel something like ripping the back of my spine

D   what I want you to do first then is to press down with your feet against my hands press down hard (.) OK now pull up against my fingers (.) can you press your feet together press your knees apart (.) just relax while I do your reflexes which are fine (.) can you bend your knees

P   oh

D   yes OK take your time (.) now keep them as they are while I just try and straighten your legs (.) right now let your feet come down that's it (.) I'm going to do the work if you can try and relax and tell me when it gets too uncomfortable

[*passage omitted*]

D   ... I'm sure this is a muscle tear because it's typical of them that er the time you do it you don't feel much it's often overnight that the pain steadily develops ... so the first thing is rest (.) secondly I'll give you some painkillers they don't speed up the healing process it's just to make life comfortable for you while it's healing (.) now it's

P   what is it is it like a thing I've got with my spine or

D   it's a torn muscle in your back yeh it should recover

P   you wouldn't think it was so painful would you

D   oh no it is but it's all right as long as you don't move as soon as you move it'll try and go into spasm to stop you using those muscles you've injured

P   how long will it take to um

D   I think you're going to be off work at least a week

[*passage omitted*]

D   if you need a signing off note to go back to I'll sign it

P   it's fine they usually don't ask for ones I just tell them what's wrong

D   just see how you get on

P   OK

D	good
P	thanks very much
D	bye
P	bye

(Source: cited by Geoff Thomson in paper 'Linking Context and Systems'
at 8th Euro-International Systemic Function Workshop, Nottingham, 1996)

Transcript 27: doctor and child patient interview

The eight-year-old child has cerebral palsy and is being examined by the
paediatrician to identify her broad educational needs

D	let me look in your ear (.) do you have a monkey in your ear
C	[*laughing*] no
D	no (.) let's see … I see … a birdie
C	[*laughing*] no
D	[*smiling*] no
[*passage omitted*]	
D	OK all right now let me (.) let me see what I can find in there [*examining child's stomach*] (.) is there peanut butter and jelly (.) wait a minute
C //	no [*giggles*]
D //	no peanut butter and jelly in there
C	no
D	bend your legs up a little bit … that's right (.) OK OK any peanut butter and jelly in here
C //	no
D	no no there's nothing in there (.) is your spleen palpable over there
C //	no [*giggles*]

(Source: cited in Tannen, 1993)

COMMENTARY Both transcripts can be analysed using the history-taking/physical
examination/diagnosis/management model.

ACTIVITY 30

Examine each stage and note examples of exchange structure (adjacency pairs and three-part exchanges), use of declaratives and imperatives. The lexis is also interesting – look at examples of register change when the doctor is talking to the adult patient (Transcript 26) and the child patient (Transcript 27), and suggest explanations.

Classroom talk

Classroom talk readily fits into the category of public talk. Although lessons are structured and planned in advance, and methods of imparting knowledge and skills are learnt strategies, the ways that individual teachers and pupils interact in the classroom with each other (whatever age the pupils) remain predominantly spontaneous and unplanned. As we have already seen in Chapter 2, Coulthard and Sinclair's model of classroom interaction is particularly useful, with its focus on the three-part exchange (initiation, response, feedback – IRF), and its differentiation between

kinds of moves. Apart from opening and closing moves, these may
include:

- teacher inform
- teacher direct
- teacher elicit
- pupil elicit
- teacher inform
- teacher check
- teacher re-initiate or elicit
- teacher re-initiate from wrong answer
- teacher require multiple/class response
- teacher reinforce
- teacher repeat.

Although these seem complicated, it should be possible to identify all or
most of these structures in the data below.

Transcript 28: extract from beginning of dance school lesson
*The ballet class is taken by a teacher **T**. The children are aged 3–4 and
whether they respond together or as individuals they are identified as **C**. **Miss B**
is a young teacher observing the class*

T	OK let's do the toaster game (.) listen (.) put your toes in the toaster and you toast toast toast (.) toast (.) toast pops up toast pops down (.) what comes next
C	hands
T	what about your knees (.) what do we do with them
C	like this
C	straight
T	straight (.) good (.) reach over (.) put y . . . our hands in the toaster and you toast toast toast (.) toast pops up toast pops down (.) what's next
C	heads heads heads
T	good (.) put your head in the toaster and you toast toast toast (.) toast pops up toast pops down (.) one thing left
C	bodies bodies bodies
T	shhh (.) put your bodies in the toaster and you toast toast toast (.) toast pops up toast pops down (.) give me a shake (.) sit on the floor nicely (.) G— (.) can you show us how to sit down properly (.) good (.) one knee two knees bottom (.) S— sit down please
C	look
T	wait a minute I've got to check my tape
C	look (.) a cat
T	legs straight
C	point toes point toes
C	S— S—
T	wait a minute girls (.) lay down
C	lay down lay down
T	shhh (.) on your backs
C	I've hurt my knee
T	that's OK it will get better soon
C	lay down R—
T	come on (.) point these toes hard (.) good (.) hands to the side (.) good (.) that's it (.) naughty toes now

C	naughty toes
T	good (.) into a circle
C	R— R—
T	now listen shh (.) come on (.) quiet (.) than you (.) that's not a circle is it (.) stand still (.) K— her name is Miss B—
C	Miss B—
T	are you going to show her how nicely you can dance (.) no talking (.) turn around so you are looking at someone's back (.) arms in *bras bas* (.) feet (.) C— (.) when the music stops we will move around (.) OK arms in *demi second* run quick (.) march with the band (.) shhh no noise (.) remember to point . . .

(Source: Amber Brown)

Transcript 29: extract from dance school lesson

*This ballet lesson is with children aged 8–10. The teacher **T** is preparing them for an examination. **H**, **L** and **D** are identified, the other children are referred to as **C**. **Miss B** is observing*

T	line up by the door and then walk to Miss B— who will be the examiner for today (.) introduce yourself and give her your syllabus
H	do we have to
T	yes H— you need to practise
	[*children introduce themselves and then stand beside barre*]
T	what do you have to remember
L	to stand still with arms in *bras bas* until told to begin
T	good L— (.) exercise one *plies* (.) what do you have to remember in *plies*
C	don't stick your bum out
T	I think remember your posture sounds better [*class giggles*] settle down I'm going to let the tape run now (.) so you need to concentrate [*class moans under breath*] do you want to pass your exam
C	yes
T	then work explain what a *tendu* is D—
D	to point
T	when you point your foot to the front what do you do
C	lead with your heel and bring it back with your toe
T	well done (.) now everyone show me (.) good (.) what common faults are found in jumps
C	sticking your bum out
T	bad posture yes (.) and what is the term for jump
C	*sauter*
T	good (.) now we are going to clap a polka beat . . .

(Source: Amber Brown)

COMMENTARY The difference between the two lessons is that the children's responses in Transcript 28 are accompanied by actions, whereas the interaction in Transcript 29 is prior to action. The older pupils are being tested on their knowledge of technique and terminology, the children's responses are predominantly non-verbal.

ACTIVITY 31

Look at the variations of the three-part exchange in each transcript – which is the most frequently used pattern? What differences do you see between the children's lexical choice and length of turn in each lesson extract?

Transcript 30: extract from classroom lesson

*The extract is from a 'presentation lesson' on geography in an Australian high school. **T** is the teacher, **C** is the class, **Px**, **Py**, **M** and **Pz** are individual pupils*

T	right we're going on (.) shush (.) we're going on from (.) now today (.) when we looked at topographic maps and we looked at grid references (.) we tried to figure out how we can locate places on the surface of the earth (.) using a grid reference (.) a quick revision of that (.) what are the line – what are the lines that run up and down our map called
C	[*in chorus*] eastings
T	hands up thank you
Px	eastings
T	eastings (.) very good (.) lines that run across our map are called what [*allows no time for response*] hands up
C	[*in chorus*] northings
Py	what an interesting name
T	right we'll stop that (.) again while I ask for hands up
Pz	northings
T	now (.) hands up please if you can give me the rule in relation to looking up a grid reference ... M—
M	eastings before northings
T	right (.) eastings before northings (.) very good (.) now (.) today we're going to look at some of the characteristics of topographic maps (.) which enable us not only to look at exact locations but also to look at land form (.) OK (.) landform refers simply to the ... now what's wrong
Px	um (.) this map
Py	miss we started a new topic the other day
T	it's not yours
Py	we were on map of Australia
T	oh forget about that map (.) now the map I am showing you here is a topographic map (.) it shows you our eastings and northings (.) our grid lines (.) it is also showing us land use patterns (.) it's showing us where different things occur on the surface of the earth

(Source: cited by Ruqaiya Hasan in paper 'Speaking with Reference to Context' at 8th Euro-International Systemic Function Workshop, Nottingham, 1996)

ACTIVITY 32

What is interesting about this interaction is the teacher's relationship with the class.

1 Identify the places where the normal three-part exchange pattern (IRF) is disrupted. How is it repaired?

2 Assess the effectiveness of this lesson extract as a means of communicating information and/or eliciting knowledge.

Courtroom language

The language of the courtroom reflects the professional relationship between lawyer and defendant. It takes place in the public domain and characteristically combines a predictable discourse structure with unpredictable responses from the defendant.

The exchange structure pattern occurs frequently, using adjacency pairs and three-part moves. Sandra Harris (1989) analyses a range of magistrate-defendant courtroom exchanges in her paper 'Defendant resistance to power and control in court', which provides the data below.

Transcript 31: magistrate and defendant

*The magistrate **M** is continuing to ask the defendant **D** about his refusal to pay adequate support to his wife*

M   do you think that it is a reasonable thing that a wife and your child shall be without your support whilst you enjoy the additional pleasure of colour – in television in your home (3) does that seem a reasonable thing to do (3)

D   depends upon which way you look at it don't it

M   well looking at it from any reasonable point of view – is it reasonable for anyone to have the pleasure and the uh – luxury of a colour television set when a wife and child could be going without food (6) whichever way you look at it is that reasonable (3)

D   well I don't know because if I didn't have a colour telly I'd just spend my time – in the pubs then wouldn't I

M   well you're not forced to do it – I don't have a colour television and I don't spend my time in the pubs – there's no compulsion to make you go to the pub because you don't have a colour television (3) besides if you spent your time in the pubs you'd only have a pint to – to – a pint a week to drink

D [ ]   yeh but then I'd be forced into having more wouldn't I

M   you wouldn't be forced into anything – nobody can force anybody to drink anything

D [ ]   no I don't agree with you – don't agree with you

(Source: Harris, cited in Coleman, 1989)

COMMENTARY   What is interesting about this exchange is that the magistrate's questions (propositions) are being rejected by the defendant, who counters with his own questions. This changes the exchange structure from an adjacency pair pattern to an argument-based debate. This may seem inappropriate in a context where the defendant is actually a law breaker! (His discourse skills in using tag questions and offering his own propositions may cause him trouble, Harris later comments.)

ACTIVITY 33

Look at the relationship of lexis to the power balance of the exchange, and find evidence to decide who holds the power linguistically.

Talking in public: the media

Radio and television provide multiple examples of unplanned talking in public. These include chat shows, phone-ins, discussions, interviews (with celebrities and private individuals), documentaries, commentaries of various kinds (especially sports commentaries), as well as the spontaneous comments of presenters, disc jockeys, weather forecasters and even news readers. All these genres include unplanned talking, but nevertheless adhere broadly to their expected generic structures, as we have already observed in relation to service encounters and classroom interaction. For example, the characteristic form of the celebrity interview (introduction, biographical outline, questioning about past, present and future, thanks and closure) is readily recognisable. Register and levels of formality may vary widely, but each genre of 'media talk' will have its own GSP (generic structure potential; see p52), its own recognisable obligatory and optional elements, in varying proportions. Our investigation focuses on four genres of media talk – the chat show, the public debate, sports commentary and the radio phone-in.

Chat show

The chat show is a relatively recent, highly popular and predominantly televisual genre. A 'personality' figure hosts a discussion, interviews guests, and chairs and monitors the spontaneous debate. Current chat show hosts range from Chris Evans, Esther Rantzen and Robert Kilroy to Oprah Winfrey, Jerry Springer and Ricki Lake. In some instances the host is the sole interviewer, in others the general public also takes part. The structure of the individual chat show may vary to a degree, but there are basic similarities. For example, all adopt an informal register and use exchange structure strategies.

Transcript 32: Robert Kilroy Silk's chat show
*Kilroy Silk (**KS**) is talking to guests (**G1**, **G2** et al) about the proposal that black British citizens should have their fare paid to return to their place of origin*

KS   hello (.) and good morning (.) Mr Bernie Grant says at least forty percent of Britain's blacks want to go back to their country of origin (.) and he believes that we should give them the cash to help them go (.) other blacks condemn him (.) for playing into the hands of the racists (0.2) [deep breath] K— (.) do you agree with (.) Bernie's proposals to allow people to go back to the country of origin uh hh and the government should pay for them to go

G1   I do

KS   why

[*passage omitted*]

G1   ... there's no future for them

KS   is that how you feel about yourself

G1   I do

KS   why and so your prime considerations are you're saying there is no work and no future (.) there's no economic reasons

G1   for economic reasons

KS   and where what would you want to move

G1   West Indies ...

[*passage omitted*]

KS   where

G1   Dominique

KS an an you'd be happy to go (.) if you were hap- if someone came along and said I will help you financially and pay (.) you would go
G1 I would yes
KS bout you M—
[*passage omitted*]
G2 no ... I'm jumpin outta the pot into the pan

(Source: NEAB standardising data)

Transcript 33: Oprah Winfrey's chat show
*Oprah Winfrey (**OW**) is discussing the fashion for hip-hop clothes among 'white kids' with guests **G1** and **G2** and with a member of the audience **A***

OW today (.) we're talking about wiggers (.) white kids that dress black (.) [*inaudible*] ...
G1 which is into hip-hop culture (.) I think that's really what the statement is
OW OK ah (.) you guys do this (.) you all obviously white guys sittin here yeah (.) yeah an uh so (.) do you wear the clothes because what ...
A because this is what we wanna wear... we used to wear dese poomers wi de fat laces everyone did it's like
OW [ ] poomers (.) he's wearing suede poomers I see (0.1) wait a minute (.) can you get a shot of th' (.) can you turn your sh foot around this way... this is this (.) would drive me crazy tryin to lace up this shoe how long does this take you to do
A five minutes
OW five minutes to do this (.) so what does this mean
[*passage omitted*]
A you just go around like that
OW so what does this say about you (0.2) S— (.) would you get this lady some water as she's having a little coughin thing here (.) you have some water (.) OK so what does this say about you (.) what do you want this to say about you
A *... they didn't tell me I had to be black to buy these shoes (.) they just told me how much they were *...
OW good point good point (0.3) *touché* [*applause*] what is a parent to do through this (.) M— you were saying as a marketing (.) expert here that (.) a lot of the parents are concerned (0.2) white parents
G2 uh (.) I think black kids felt their own style was being copied by other people
OW we have a lot of kids here today who say that (.) what is a parent to do when a child start wearing clothes (.) twelve sizes too big ... so (.) it's OK for you that your son dresses this way (.) this is
G2 [ ] I think it's wonderful (.) we're here today with (0.1) uh Tim's (.) one of Tim's best friends and his dad who are black people (.) the boys dress like this together um *...
OW do you see it as a black thing
G2 no
OW you just see it as
G2 [ ] I see it as cross culture thing
OW as a cross culture thing
G2 an I think it's marvellous

(Source: NEAB standardising data)

COMMENTARY The structure of these complex systems of exchanges can be identified to some extent: each chat show host starts with greetings ('hello and good morning') or a contextualisation ('today we're talking ...') followed by topic identification ('Mr Bernie Grant says ...') or ('... about wiggers white kids that dress black'). Then the adjacency pairs sequences begin: in Transcript 32 they follow a regular pattern; in Transcript 33 the question-answer sequences are more complex because OW comments on the answers of her guests, asks the camera-man to adjust a shot, asks an assistant to fetch a drink for a member of the audience – all as part of her turn.

ACTIVITY 34

Look at examples of opening and closing moves, exchange boundaries, topic shifts and phatic language. It is also worth examining politeness strategies, frequency of overlaps and interruptions. Is it possible to characterise the idiolect of each chat show host.

Radio phone-ins

Another kind of media talk is the radio phone-in. This can take place more or less at any time of the day or night, and functions on a similar model to the chat show, in that there is a host/presenter who may also act as a DJ. Radio phone-ins can be found on most local radio stations, on national frequencies like Radio 1, 2, 4 and 5, as well as commercial stations. The subject matter will be determined (sometimes in advance, sometimes spontaneously) by the kind of audience the radio station usually addresses. This can range from matters of national concern (*Call Nick Ross* [Radio 4] on capital punishment) to local issues ('Should a bypass be built?'), from breakfast shows (Radio 1) to programmes like *Late Night Live* and *Up all Night* (Radio 5). Time constraints mean that a caller needs to put his or her point quickly to allow others a turn: it's noticeable that on local radio people are given more generous time allocation. Just as in the wonderful television sitcom *Frasier* (about a psychiatric advice line), there is screening of callers before they get on air, so that the presenter doesn't have to cut off obscene or insulting calls too often.

The generic structure can vary from question/answer or comment/elaboration to a complex debate using a variety of structures. In an issue-focused phone-in the presenter will ask one question and callers will respond with a number of answers. In a more informal chatty phone-in, the caller will sometimes ask the presenter a question or will make a declarative statement or comment after the presenter's phatic greeting, to which the presenter must respond and elaborate. Thus the relationship between presenter and caller is rather different from normal interaction. Furthermore, although they may be talking on a one-to-one basis, a third potential interactant is always present – the radio audience. Presenters have to manage the calls as they come in, and make each caller feel that their view is important. Callers will range from the fluent and articulate to the nervous and tongue-tied, so politeness strategies are essential. (Occasionally an idiosyncratic presenter like Chris Evans gets away with being rude).

Transcript 34: extract from a phone-in programme

*This is an exchange between the presenter **H** and a caller **C** on the subject of telethons*

C   … but er I- I think we should be working at breaking down that separateness I think these (.)

H [ ]   how

C   telethons actually increase it

H   well what you're saying is that charity does

C   (.) charity does yes I mean

H [ ]   OK we- so you're (.) so you're going back to that original argument that we shouldn't have charity

C   well no um I wouldn't go that far (.) what I would like to see is

H [ ]   well how far are you going then

(Source: cited in Drew, 1994)

COMMENTARY   This short extract illustrates a phone-in debate. The caller is arguing that telethons increase separateness; the presenter reminds the caller of the original argument and then challenges ('well how far are you going then'). The presenter questions the logic of the caller and the validity of the argument. This is done by exchange structure variations.

ACTIVITY 35

1 Note the relative frequency of non-fluency features in each speaker's language.
2 Record a phone-in on local radio and another on national radio. Compare the generic structure variation, the register range, and the frequency of non-fluency features. You may wish to note the gender of the participants in each phone-in.

Sports commentaries

Sports commentaries provide good examples of public talk which has certain obligatory elements in its structure and organisation, particularly in radio broadcasting. Different sports have different requirements; for example, cricket commentaries (where there are extended pauses between actions) have different patterns of language from football commentaries, where the action tends to be fast and more or less continuous. Racing commentaries are even faster, with the commentator's voice dramatically speeding up and rising in pitch as the winning post is reached. In football commentaries in particular there are usually two commentators, providing a dual perspective on the action for the benefit of the listening audience. The GSP of football commentary tends to match the allotted time-slot: first an introductory chat describing the scene, discussing likely outcomes, commenting on players etc. Once the match begins, the aim of the commentators is to give as accurate and vivid an account of the match as possible, constrained only by the length of the broadcast. The commentary functions rather like an ongoing narrative; Labov's and Hasan's complementary theories of narrative structure may prove useful in identifying the GSP of radio football commentary.

Transcript 35: radio commentary Blackburn Rovers *v* Spartak Moscow

*Only two of the three commentators present at the match speak. These are **AG** and **ML**. **MI** is silent. The commentary starts at the very beginning of the second half*

AG still leaves Steve Sutton in the (.) er defence
ML and Steve Sutton as well (2.0)
AG as well
ML try try Chris Sutton
AG Chris Sutton oh (2.0) wake it up Greeny (.) that's what happens when you get back at half past three in the morning (.) goodness gracious and I wasn't out on the town folks (.) that was when the flight got in (2.0) Chris Sutton still on the bench goodness (.) well I'm sure he's gonna play at some stage (2.0) fifteen seconds under way in the second half Blackburn nil Spartak Moscow (.) one (.) these are the teams (.) Blackburn Rovers as er Trevor Brooking signs autographs goodness gracious I should call him in now just to embarrass him (.) Flowers is the goal keeper at fault for the goals (.)

(Source: Margaret Walker)

Transcript 36: radio commentary on Derby County *v* Coventry City (23.3.98)

*There are two commentators, **GR** and **IH**. Note that pauses have not been marked*

GR but at the moment a ball given away by Breen AND THROUGH COMES WANCHOPE AND WANCHOPE PUTS IT AND BREEN CLEARS IT OFF THE LINE well a complete mess up as Ian was talking Breen in clear possession suddenly lost the ball under his toes Wanchope was on top of him got the ball away from him straight chase to goal Ogrizovic came out Wanchope went away to the right hand side put the shot past the keeper and Breen had done the decent thing and got back and cleared it off the line out of absolutely nothing Derby nearly created an opportunity down to Breen's error and it was Breen who swept it up
[retrospective commentary after the incident]
IH well that was comic cuts wasn't it I mean 30 yards out Breen as if his shoes have suddenly filled with lead didn't they and he couldn't kick the ball at all and it was taken off him by a combination of Wanchope and Baiano and they went between them descended upon Ogrizovic he went to the floor Wanchope was forced to the side Baiano was all on his own about 8 yards out Wanchope tried to kick it into an empty goal and in the meantime Breen had got the lead out of his boots and got back and scraped it off the line but you wouldn't find that in a playground

(Source: Michael Macken)

COMMENTARY

The two commentaries differ interestingly. In Transcript 35 **AG** muddles up two players with the same last name, excuses his error, and moves into football gossip – no significant play has yet taken place. In Transcript 36 there is a real action commentary followed by an evaluation of the near goal incident. One is introductory chat, one is simultaneous narrative, one is considered assessment. We would expect these differences to be signalled linguistically.

ACTIVITY 36

Look for examples of interactive features, incomplete clauses, ellipsis, non-fluency features, evaluative lexis, register variation, phatic language, tense variation, metaphoric language. Link these features with the function and organisation of each commentary.

Broadcast debate

The final example of media language which is public and unplanned (or at least, only partially planned) is the broadcast debate, either on radio or television. This involves a number of participants, including a chair who manages the discussion, makes sure speakers are allocated turns, and provides summative or reformulatory comments as appropriate. A radio programme like *Any Questions* (BBC Radio 4) is a good example, where the audience asks a panel of speakers questions about current issues. The speakers then debate the issue, whilst the audience remains silent. Similarly in a televised public debate like *Question Time* a panel of speakers respond to questions from the audience. The major difference is that the audience is invited to participate as well as ask questions. Sometimes these responses are prepared, sometimes they are spontaneous.

From a linguistic perspective the organisation of turn-taking is the key area of interest. Langford (1994) identifies the characteristic feature of this kind of multi-party talk – each participant is both speaker and listener. As listener, the participant's level of interest and involvement may be indicated by back-channel behaviour; as speaker, the participant will either speak themselves on the topic or invite another speaker to do so. Participants' contributions may include sustained narrative or argument demonstrating their support or hostility to the propositions, and they also have to compete for available speaking turns.

Transcript 37: extract from radio debate
*The speakers are the questioner from the audience (**Sp1**), the chairman (**Sp2**) and the panel of four. Four speakers are named: Professor Halsey (**Sp4/PH**), David Willetts (**DW**), Glenda Jackson (**Sp3/GJ**) and Charles Kennedy **CK**. (The linking of speaker identification with individuals is somewhat provisional)*

Sp1 how can the Labour government believe that at sixteen a person is mature enough to decide if they are homosexual (.) get married or go to war (.) but not old enough to decide if they wish to smoke

Sp2 this is the proposal that there is (.) that the ban on teenage smoking may be raised from sixteen to eighteen (.) Professor Halsey

PH well I ... I ... wasn't aware that there was such a proposal and certainly it would be an example of the enormous distance between the legislature and common practice (.) I ... I ... I ... remember starting to smoke at age nine or ten (.) and I- I didn't even know what the law was in in those days er (.) I am now a reformed smoker and er it seems to me to be a rather stinking habit as a result of erm escaping from it and I- er hope that we will use all reasonable means to er persuade people to er be non smokers

Sp2 erm (.) Minister you are a (.) unreformed serial smoker (.) what's your view

Sp3 er I (.) I think I could question the word serial

Sp2 how many a day

Sp3 well certainly not the forty I am reported to smoke (.) erm yes I- I- I ... admit that I am as yet an (.) un- unreformed smoker (.) but I was in the House of Commons to assist in this because there are so many areas that you may not smoke (.) but I certainly didn't start at the age of sixteen or indeed at the age of nine (.) I think this is something that warrants examination given that there is a marked increase in smoking among young people and many of them way way below the age of sixteen (.) erm (.) and I think if we can assist er young people not getting into this habit which I know from bitter experience is extremely hard to break then I think we certainly should explore every possibility because we are losing too many people

Sp2 OK (.) a reminder that the question (.) the contrast that Mr Hickey pose – poses is that you can make other kinds of decisions not least you can be sent to war (.) erm at the age of 16 (.) David Willetts

DW I think it's a very good question because it does get at the – it ties in with the previous question what do we tolerate and there are (.) must be limits to (.) bossiness (.) we all instinctively (.) occasionally when there's something that comes up that we dislike (.) or we disapprove of (.) or we persuade is unhealthy think (.) oh there should be a law against it but you know if I look back on the (.) er (.) years of Conservative government some of the regrets that I have are laws that we passed that subsequently looking back were too intrusive and too heavy-handed (.) and what I think that we are already getting is another set of attempts at banning this

[*passage omitted*]

CK well I speak here as a lapsed reformed smoker er (.) and it will be my New Year resolution in a few weeks time to do something against it

Sp2 you mean not to lapse again (.) so you'll stay smoking

CK I think (.) I think leaving that sufficiently [*inaudible*] is probably a good idea

Sp4 he's very good at giving up smoking (.) he's given up lots of times

CK I think this is a daft idea (.) er (.) I think first of all the point of principle which the questioner raises is accurate

(Source: BBC Radio 4, Any Questions*)*

COMMENTARY

This particular topic provokes mainly personal comments from the panel rather than a debate on matters of principle. **PH** is a reformed smoker, **Sp3** (probably **GJ**) still smokes, **DW** gives no information on his personal status but focuses on the issue of individual liberty, **CK** is a smoker who can't give up. The extract mainly consists of statements not arguments. In this multi-party talk the chair (**Sp2**) manages the discussion by inviting people to speak to the question, but it takes some time before the central issue is focused on.

ACTIVITY 37

Look at individual idiolects of the speakers in terms of lexical choice and non-fluency features.

Note the management of turn-taking and the use of adjacency pairs.

Talking in public: communicating information

We are all familiar with public announcements, ranging from information about trains, planes and buses over the public address system, to weather forecasting, and specialised language used by people in particular occupations, such as air traffic control, CB radio, police, fire and ambulance services. Information is communicated according to circumstances, as they arise, and to that extent its communication can be described as unplanned. In some cases the audience is the general public needing specific information (ie travellers, farmers, sailors); in other cases there are direct exchanges between the information provider and the information receiver. Each information-communicating spoken genre has a characteristic format, usually modelling exchange structure patterns. For example, the airline pilot hardly needs phatic language to receive or communicate information from air traffic control. David Crystal calls these genres restricted languages, and points out that in *Seaspeak* (international language of the sea) standard phrases are used to avoid ambiguity; certain normal interaction language features are not permitted (tag questions, intonational questions); and there are 'fixed syntactic and lexical routines' (Crystal, 1987). What is paradoxical about these public information-communicating genres is that they remain rigid in form, whether monologic or dialogic (planned), and yet must be flexible enough to respond to changing situations (unplanned).

Transcript 38: language of air traffic control – radiotelephony

*The following extracts were recorded in the fields of general aviation and commercial aviation. In both transcripts the aircraft is **A** and ground control **ATC**. (Glossary: 'roger' means I have received all of your last transmission; 'squawk' means set the transponder mode and code as instructed)*

General Aviation

A1 Leicester radio good afternoon this is G-BLZP

ATC station calling say again

A1 Leicester this is G-BLZP how do you read

ATC G-ZP readability 4 pass your message

A1 G-BLZ is a Cessna 152 student pilot on board out of East Midlands bound overhead Eyebrooke and (.) er (.) eventually Sywell just passing to the east of your field and requesting traffic information I'm currently at 2400 feet on the barn

ATC er (.) roger we're using 28 left hand QNH 1028 and no conflicting traffic in your area

A1 you're using 1028 and nothing known to interfere thank you very much I'll be in touch

ATC we're using 28 left hand QNH 1028

A1 28 left hand 1028 G-ZP
[*passage omitted*]

A1 I'd like to change frequency now to Sywell on 122.7

ATC 122.7 roger squawk 7000

A1 squawk and thanks for your help G-ZP

Commercial Aviation

ATC	AIRFRANCE 0646 climb flight level 290
A1	AIRFRANCE climbing 290 thank you
A2	London afternoon MIDLAND 58 heading 335
ATC	MIDLAND 58 good afternoon climb flight level 180
A2	flight level 180 MIDLAND 58
ATC	SPEEDBIRD 32 GOLF contact London on 131.05 routing direct to Pole Hill
A3	131.05 direct Pole Hill SPEEDBIRD 32 GOLF
ATC	SHUTTLE 75 heading 340
A4	340 for SHUTTLE 75
A5	SHUTTLE 340 approaching flight level 200
ATC	SHUTTLE 40 thank you climb now flight level 280
A5	climb flight level 280 SHUTTLE 40
A1	AIRFRANCE 046 maintaining level 290
ATC	AIRFRANCE 046 roger
ATC	UK 618 continue present heading until advised
A6	continue present heading until advised UK 618 and heading 325
ATC	MIDLAND 58 climb flight level 280
A2	climb level 280 MIDLAND 58

[*passage omitted*]

ATC	AIRFRANCE 046 contact London 131.05 goodbye

[*passage omitted*]

A7	London good afternoon BRITTANNIA 444B passing 260 descending flight level 200
ATC	BRITTANNIA 44B thank you
ATC	UK 618 contact Manchester 124.2 goodbye
A6	124.2 goodbye
ATC	SHUTTLE 40 direct to Trent call London 128.05 goodbye
A5	128.05 direct to Trent SHUTTLE 40 bye
ATC	MIDLAND 58 contact London 131.05 goodbye
A2	131.05 MIDLAND 58 goodbye
A7	SHUTTLE 444B reaching flight level 200
ATC	SHUTTLE 444B roger

(Source: Alex Lanterna)

COMMENTARY   Each turn is part of an adjacency pair in both transcripts. These adjacency pairs include: initiation/response; statement/acknowledgement; question/answer; instruction/acknowledgement; greeting/farewell etc. For safety purposes it is essential that every statement, question, instruction from ground control is acknowledged by the aircraft being guided through airspace.

ACTIVITY 38

Find examples of each kind of adjacency pair in the transcripts. Note too the field-specific lexis.

List examples of formulaic jargon ('roger', 'flight level', 'heading').

5 Talking In Public: Planned Speech

There is a significant difference between talking more or less spontaneously in the kind of public contexts outlined in the previous chapter, and talking in public when what you say is planned in advance. Planned talking can differ in form, structure and lexical choice, and the contexts in which it occurs are also different from those for everyday talk. However, because most people are naturally spontaneous talkers, the idea of planning exactly what to say can be uncomfortable, even alienating on occasion, unless we are practised public speakers. Planned talking in public is something we all have to do from time to time, with varying degrees of grace. If the audience is familiar, it may help, but it may make matters worse! Examples of planned talking in public include: family celebrations (which tend to require speeches); oral presentations (increasingly used to assess performance in both educational and occupational contexts); and speaking on behalf of community groups, volunteer associations, sports clubs, social clubs etc. If asked to speak in public, most people plan what they are going to say, (few 'funny stories' are spontaneous, unless you're a professional comedian). Oddly enough, despite this anxious planning when we have to speak in pulic, the highest praise for a public speaker is that he or she sounded 'completely natural' (ie unplanned). Like the virtuoso musician, the most eloquent speakers in the public arena must *appear* effortless.

But how 'natural' *is* naturally sounding speech? Analysing different kinds of unplanned (or natural talk) in Chapters 3 and 4 demonstrated not just the rich variation of form and structure in talk, but also its vulnerability to individual speakers' personality quirks. We all have our own idiolect, warts (or non-fluency features) and all! Should a successful public speaker include all these features in order to appear 'natural'?

Planned or scripted talk then must accomplish two things, one positive, the other negative. It must be so polished or seemingly accurate in its reproduction of naturally occurring talk that the audience is totally convinced; and it must *not* reproduce any of the muddle of normal exchanges with their non-fluency features (or only occasionally, for a warming touch of realism). In our investigations of a range of planned public talk, these criteria, as well as the more standard discourse techniques of analysis will be applied. We shall investigate planned public speaking in legal and political contexts; media genres like soap opera, game shows and stand-up comedy; news broadcasting and documentary; the language of religion (liturgy, sermon etc) and the academic lecture.

In this chapter data taken from scripted texts will be described as *extracts*; data taken directly from planned spoken texts will be described as *transcripts*.

Planned speaking in public: political and legal genres

Political speech

The political speech is a familiar genre, which may or may not involve audience response, depending on the context. Whether in parliament or at a local political meeting, members of the audience may well interject comments, ask rhetorical questions, or otherwise interrupt the flow of the planned speech. Whatever the context, skilful speakers can deflect or even exploit audience comment as part of their argument (eg Peter Sellers' parodic version of a political meeting: *Voice from floor*: 'What about the workers?' *Speaker from platform*: 'What about the workers indeed sir!'). Thus the political speech, or the political interview where opportunity has been given to prepare answers in advance, is a flexible and powerful instrument for persuasion. This is not the appropriate place or indeed book to explore the complex and important area of rhetoric. It is sufficient to say here that the persuasive element in talk is probably as central as its generic structure potential, and that persuasion to a greater or lesser degree is part of all our talking, public or private, planned or unplanned.

The following extracts from a political speech and a political interview are not transcriptions, so there can be no clear indications of how they were spoken, apart from the obvious links between punctuation and pauses for breath. Extract 1 is from Martin Luther King's speech on 28 August 1963, when he addressed an audience of 210,000 at the Lincoln Memorial in Washington, a culminating moment in the civil rights movement.

Extract 1 from 'I have a dream . . .' by Martin Luther King

Five score years ago, a great American [*Abraham Lincoln*], in whose symbolic shadow we stand, signed the Emancipation Proclamation. This momentous decree came as a great beacon of hope to millions of Negro slaves who had been seared in the flames of withering injustice. It came as a joyous daybreak to end the long night of captivity.

But one hundred years later, we must face the tragic fact that the Negro is still not free. One hundred years later, the life of the Negro is still sadly crippled by the manacles of segregation and the chains of discrimination. One hundred years later, the Negro lives on a lonely island of poverty in the midst of a vast ocean of material prosperity. One hundred years later, the Negro is still languished in the corners of American society and finds himself an exile in his own land. So we have come here today to dramatize an appalling condition . . .

... I say to you today, my friends, that in spite of the difficulties and frustrations of the moment I still have a dream. It is a dream deeply rooted in the American dream.

I have a dream that one day this nation will rise up and live out the true meaning of its creed: 'We hold these truths to be self-evident that all men are created equal'.

I have a dream that one day on the red hills of Georgia the sons of former slaves will be able to sit down together at the table of brotherhood.

I have a dream that one day even the state of Mississippi, a desert state sweltering with the heat of injustice and oppression, will be an oasis of freedom and justice.

I have a dream that my four little children will one day live in a nation where they will not be judged by the color of their skin but by the content of their character.

I have a dream ...

COMMENTARY In a scripted speech there is much more opportunity for planned linguistic strategies than in a spontaneous one. King's aim here is to persuade his audience that justice has not yet been granted to the black American citizen. He uses a range of rhetorical strategies (lexical, grammatical and syntactical) to create a powerful image of his dream for his people.

ACTIVITY 39

Look at the metaphoric language – what effects are achieved by the kind of images used and how do they support his argument? Look for examples of syntactic patterning (repetition, triple structures, syntactic parallelism). How does King involve his audience (look for personal pronouns, imperatives, interrogatives)?

Parliamentary speech

Extract 2 scripted parliamentary answer
*The extract is taken from the official written record of an exchange between the then Prime Minister, Mrs Thatcher (**PM**), and a Conservative MP, Mr Latham, (**ML**). The question and answer sequence seems to be spontaneous, but closer examination suggests it is carefully planned*

ML While continuing to implement the policies which have been approved by the electorate on three occasions, will my Right Honourable Friend confirm that successful governments must always be responding and listening to the real aspirations of the people?

PM Yes. That is why under the ten-year-old policies of Conservative governments we have created more wealth than ever before, have spread it more widely than ever before, have higher standards of social services than ever before, and have a higher reputation than ever before. Yes, we have indeed been listening. I believe that these are the real aspirations of the British people.

(Source: cited in Cockcroft and Cockcroft, 1992)

Extract 3 from *Yes Minister*

This is a parodic version of a more confrontational political interview from the first comedy series Yes Minister. *Jim Hacker, an anxious but ambitious Cabinet Minister, is being interviewed on television*

Int   Now Minister – are you laying the foundations of the police state
JH   You know – I'm glad you asked me that question
Int   Well Minister – could we have the answer
JH   Well yes of course – I'm just about to give it to you – if I may – uh – yes – as I said I'm glad you asked me that question because [*pause*] it's a question [*pause*] a lot of people are asking – because a lot of people want to know the answer to it – and let's be quite clear about this – without beating about the bush – the plain fact of the matter is – that it's a very important question indeed – and people have a right to know
Int   Minister – we haven't yet had the answer
JH   I'm sorry – what was the question

(Source: cited by Harris in Scannell, 1991)

COMMENTARY   In both extracts the speakers aim to present themselves and their points in the best possible light. Both use the exchange structure pattern; in both cases the questions are prepared. The parliamentary tradition of asking such prepared questions is frequently used to give the Government and the Prime Minister the chance to blow their own trumpet about their achievements in office. The lexical choice is strongly positive ('approved on three occasions', 'successful' etc); in both extracts political jargon is used frequently ('implement the policies', 'laying the foundations', 'people have a right to know').

ACTIVITY 40

1   Look for rhetorical strategies in the **PM**'s answer (eg triple structures, syntactic parallelism, repetition). Note too the deliberately vague language of Extract 3, where **JH** says nothing at all very elaborately; list the collocations, colloquialisms and euphemisms. Are there any conversational implicatures in the extracts?

2   Study a televised parliamentary session when a major government speech is coming up (check the broadsheet papers); or attend a public meeting about local issues and study one or more speakers. In both cases analyse parts of the speeches.

Language of the law

The language of court procedure is public and planned, and though written records must be kept, talking is central. A suspect is informed of his or her rights; witnesses are cross-examined; prosecution and defence speeches are made; the judge's summing-up is offered and the sentence declared. We shall look at the legal judgment, an example of highly planned legal language, intended for the broadest public audience, presented as spoken language but set down in written form. This judgment is the expression of opinion on a matter of legal principle by a law lord to the House of Lords, the upper chamber of Parliament. What is interesting from our perspective is that it reads like rather formal talk.

Extract 4 from a judgment made by Lord Hailsham

R v Maloney

LORD HAILSHAM OF MARYLEBONE LC
My Lords, for the reasons which appear in the speech about to be delivered by my noble and learned friend Lord Bridge of Harwich, which I have had the pleasure of reading in draft and with which I agree, the disposal of this case cannot be in doubt. The appeal must be allowed. The verdict of murder must be set aside. A verdict of manslaughter must be substituted. The case must be remitted to the Court of Appeal (Criminal Division) to determine the appropriate sentence. The case must be listed for hearing at the earliest possible date. The appellant has been in custody since November 1981, since the date of his conviction on a life sentence for murder, which, on any view, must be treated as unsafe and unsatisfactory . . .

(Source: cited in Maley, OPSL, 1989)

COMMENTARY What is interesting about this judgment is that it includes interpersonal language (find some examples), and particularly verbs expressing possibility (modal auxiliaries like should, must, might). Note the legal lexis and the use of the passive voice.

ACTIVITY 41

Study a courtroom scene on film or television, and analyse the rhetorical strategies used by lawyers. (Reminder: you are not allowed to record actual court proceedings in the UK.)

Media talk: scripted genres

Scripted or planned talk in the media can be found in a variety of genres including soap opera, situation comedy and comedy shows (aimed to entertain), as well as news broadcasting, weather forecasts and documentaries (aimed to inform). Some genres (sitcom, soap opera and news broadcasts) are entirely scripted; some (comedy shows or weather forecasting) seem spontaneous but are actually scripted; other genres (documentaries, special reports) may include a combination of scripted and non-scripted items. The aim of all these genres of media talk, however, is to seem as natural and spontaneous as possible. We shall now look at some examples of these various scripted genres, to see how successfully they reproduce naturally occurring talk.

Soap operas

Soap opera began in America in the 1930s as radio serials sponsored by soap powder manufacturers. They were targeted mainly at women, the usual purchasers of the product. Soap opera translated easily to television as the medium developed, and today virtually all soap opera in the UK is televised, apart from *The Archers* (started daily radio transmission 1 January 1951). Current soap operas include *Eastenders, Brookside* and *Coronation Street*, as well as the Australian soaps, *Neighbours* and *Home and Away*. Because the setting is usually a small town or community, with the focus on a few key families, most of the scripted dialogue is in the genre of casual conversation, with some occasional service encounters, classroom interaction, and other professional or occupational encounters (doctor, lawyer, social worker, minister, police, for example). The key families tend to include teenagers and young adults as well as parents, hence there are opportunities for teenage slang (no taboo language, however). There is often a local venue where all the characters can meet informally to progress the plot (pub, club, corner shop, coffee shop). The linguistic expectations are of more or less standard usage, with some regional variation in accent, for example *Coronation Street*, and constantly updated lexis including slang. *The Archers* even provides farming information via the plot, and has been used for Ministry of Agriculture propaganda. Other plot issues include relationships, teenage problems, and medical, social and economic difficulties. The language of soaps is intended to sound entirely lifelike and realistic. By looking at two short extracts from *Coronation Street* and from *The Archers* we should be able to see how close 'soap' talk is to real talk.

Transcript 39: *Coronation Street*
*The following exchange is between **F** (Fiona) and **A** (Audrey) who is buying Fiona's hairdressing business*

A   come on, give me the little fellow (.) you go and gerron with your packing

F   would you

A   of course I would (.) come on my sweetheart (.) the last time (.) you come and sit with me for a bit

F   you are going to be able to get the money on time (.) aren't you (.) I mean

A   I know it is love (.) I mean (.) there's hardly anything needs doing to it [*laughs*]

F   there's nothing needs doing to it (.) I spent a fortune on it only a year ago

A   err yes I know but

F [ ]   you're not trying to get this on the cheap now are you

A   Fiona (.) come on (.) of course I'm not [*laughs*]

F   it's a good little business this (.) and I do not want to get into haggling especially with you

A   oh please don't worry Fiona (.) I won't leave you dangling on a string (.) I'll let you know as soon as I can honestly (.) let you know as soon as I can

Transcript 40: *The Archers*

*Ruth (**R**) and David Archer (**D**) are thirty-something and work on the family farm. **R** has special responsibility for the dairy herd, **D** has broader overall responsibilities. They are discussing a recent calving. The exchange is also significant for the future plot*

D	successful delivery
R	yeah (.) I wish they all came out so easily
D	any more due
R	mmm (.) she won't be long over there (.) see
D	oh yeah
R	let's hope she drops it at a civilised hour (.) I've had enough of midnight calvings for one week
D	well I'll go and tell her to shall I
R	if only it were that simple

[*cow moos*]

D	are you OK to carry on here
R	yeah (.) there (.) I think you're ready to go and see your mum (.) that's it
D	well I'll help Debbie and Bert with the sugar beet if that's OK
R	yeah sure (.) what time will you be finished over there
D	well (.) errm (.) it's hard to say (.) could be late
R	I'll cancel the dinner date at Grey Gables shall I
D	erm
R	maybe when calving's over
D	yeah (.) you're on (.) in the meantime how does prawn biryani sound
R	sounds good to me
D	yeah (.) well (.) I'll go into Borchester and pick one up later shall I
R	that'll be great (.) don't fancy cooking
D	ah (.) I didn't think you would
R	I'd like to open a bottle of wine and collapse in a heap

COMMENTARY   Many of the normal features of casual conversation are absent; no interruptions, only one overlap and a few incomplete utterances and non-fluency features. You are unlikely to be aware of their absence because we ignore most non-fluency features in everyday conversation. To include them in a script would both waste time and slow down the interaction.

ACTIVITY 42

1 Look for examples of tag questions, back-channel behaviour, ellipsis, colloquial lexis which it seems do have to be there to create authenticity (at least partially). Are there any significant differences between the 'voices' of *Coronation Street* (television) and those of *The Archers* (radio)?

2 Choose a soap opera which appeals to the group you are working with and jointly write an episode, ensuring that you use the data above as a resource or model for your own script. Perform a dramatic reading for the class to discuss as an example of a scripted text.

Game show

This popular comedy genre has a variety of formats, usually involving a single celebrity figure quizzing members of the public who have volunteered to take part in the show before a live studio audience. Some kind of reward is given to the participants, which can be money, goods, or in the case of *Blind Date*, a 'romantic holiday for two' (the additional company of the film crew not being mentioned). What is interesting about this genre is not only its planned and public nature, but its fixed structure and formulaic language, which satisfactorily fulfil the expectations of the audience every week. There is some modest opportunity for individuals to make their mark (through their repartee usually), despite the otherwise predictable catchphrases and knee-jerk audience responses.

Blind Date is an enormously popular example of this genre, with Cilla Black the celebrity presenter. Male volunteers have to select a female 'blind date' from a choice of three (as in the extract below), and a female volunteer chooses a male 'blind date' similarly. Previous 'romantic couples' report on their blind date experiences in the course of the show.

Transcript 41: extract from *Blind Date*
*Cilla Black (**CB**) is introducing the show and the three female contestants (**F1**, **F2** and **F3**). The male questioner (**M1**) asks each for their response to the same question (three questions in total)*

CB   … we'll also catch up with Steve and Donna-Marie playing around in sunny Portugal [*audience cheers*] but right now lets meet three lovely girls looking for a blind date so come in the girls [*applause and signature tune reprise*] hi girls

F1, 2 & 3   hi Cilla hi Cilla

CB   hello number 1 what's your name and where do you come from

F1   hi Cilla my name's Joanne and I'm from Lancashire [*audience cheers*]

CB   our Joanne from Lancashire what do you do Joanne

F1   I'm a care assistant Cilla looking after the elderly

CB   aah will you look after me when I get old

F1   I certainly will Cilla [*laughs with audience*] I'd love to

CB   now there is a certain type of fella is there not that you adore

F1   certainly Cilla a Scotsman [*audience whoops and cheers*] [*inaudible*]

CB   as you can hear it's full of Scots out there [*audience laughter*] now what drives you wild about a Scotsman

F1   ooh the accents the accent and their kilts [*CB inaudible*] because I love them

CB   oh you do I can't promise you a Scottie tonight all right but I can promise you a good time enjoy Blind Date Joanne [*audience cheers*] hello number 2 what's your name and where do you come from

F2   hi Cilla my name's Nicole and I come from Stoke on Trent [*audience cheers and whistles*]

CB   many happy memories of Stoke I've had now what do you do love

F2   I'm a student midwife

CB   oh a student midwife I mean have you actually helped in delivering a baby

F2 [ ]   yes I have yes only recently I had a bit of a funny experience actually because there was a lady it was holding my hand that tight that she actually stopped the circulation in my hand [*audience laughter*] so I thought maybe I don't want children after all maybe this isn't what I want but after the baby beautiful baby girl was born it brought tears to my eyes and it's restored my faith [*inaudible*]

CB   oh I hope so too do you know I'm looking at that those lovely features there now I know you were born and bred in Stoke good old Stoke but I mean your parents weren't were they

F2   no they're both from er Chilean South America

CB   Chile South America [*audience cheers*] can you speak Spanish then
F2   I can . . .
[*passage omitted*]
M1   here we go here we go first question sorry um hello ladies
F1, 2 & 3   hello Duncan
M1   whe hey how you're doing here we go here we go first question right I'm a proud Scot all right and tonight in case you havenae gathered I'm wearing the kilt which for me is a symbol of Scotland what is it that makes you think of Scotland and that question goes to number 1 please
F1   well a Scottish accent has always made me go really weak at the knees but after tonight Duncan when I think of Scotland I'll only think of you [*audience roars approval*]
M1   thank you number 1 same again to number 2 please
F2   well for me what reminds me of Scotland has got to be er Scotch whisky because er when we have a wee dram together you'll find that I've got a very free spirit [*groans and applause from audience*]
M1   er number 3 please
F3   when I think of bonny Scotland [*M1 inaudible*] I think of the Loch Ness so if you pick me tonight I'll guarantee you'll have a monster of a time [*audience whoops, applauds and roars*]

ACTIVITY 43

The purpose of the 'interviews' is to introduce the contestants to the audience (studio and television) and to make them seem individuals. This conceals the formulaic nature of the show.

1 What evidence can you find that the contestants have prepared their responses a) to Cilla Black and b) to the male questioner?

What evidence is there of spontaneous unprepared talking? What is the function of the studio audience in the show?

2 Study a number of game shows and compare the discourse structure of the exchanges between presenter/game show host and volunteer participant.

Situation comedy

Situation comedy is another genre which transfers easily between radio and television (and vice versa) though the BBC broadcasts fewer radio sitcoms. On British television early sitcoms like *Till Death do us Part*, *Steptoe* and *Dad's Army* were followed by *Fawlty Towers*, *Men Behaving Badly*, *Absolutely Fabulous* and *Blackadder*. Two of the most successful sitcoms today are American products – *Frasier* and *Friends*.

What is a situation comedy? It's not a drama, nor is it a serial like soap operas. The aim is to make the audience laugh; characters 'can, and should be, as rounded as any characters in a television play. But the pressure is on them to say amusing things more or less all the time' (Brian Cooke, *Writing Comedy for Television* (1983), p1). Each episode consists of a series of short scenes and is self-contained. The characters are normal people in recognisable real-life situations. The first episode of any new sitcom will need to establish the characters and set up possible plot lines for later episodes (the pressure to make people laugh as this evolves is central). In other words, the sitcom is 'a playlet with laughs'. From the linguistic point of view we shall expect the features of normal casual conversation. Making the audience laugh, however, is achieved by a range of linguistic strategies: *misunderstanding* (a key word or phrase is misinterpreted); *cross-purpose talking* (two characters think they're talking about the same thing, but they're not); *the one-liner* ('I think I've just sprained my imagination'); *the running gag* (a joke alluded to in each episode); *the frustration routine* (eg one character in a hurry, being delayed by situation or another character); innuendo (risque humour); *exaggeration* (character with a cold sees it as a dramatic illness), as well as *visual gags* (banana skins etc).

Extract 5 from *Absolutely Fabulous*

E (Edina) is an outrageously extravagant PR executive, obsessed with fashion; S (Saffron), her serious-minded student daughter, attempts to keep her mother under control; P (Patsy), a fashion editor, E's best friend and fellow hedonist, into fast cars, champagne and men. Edina's mother (M), cosily unaware of fashion, supports Saffron and constantly deflates Edina's self-dramatising antics with gently barbed truths. The scripted extracts below are from different episodes, Morocco *and* Poor

Morocco

S	Marrakech? Why are you going to Marrakech?
E	Well, for the fashion shoot, sweetie.
S	Why do you have to go there?
E	Oh, God. Who are you? Magnus Makerson [*sic*] all of a sudden? Hands on buzzers – 'I don't know. Pass'. Just because ... all right?
P	No, Eddy. Eddy, not 'just because'. This is my job. I mean, these things aren't decided at random.
E	Yeah. No-no-no.
S	It's supposed to be really beautiful out there.
E	Well, you know, darling, we spent all those Christmases out there, don't you remember, when you were a child?
S	You never took me. You always left me here with Gran.
E	I know but, you got the postcards, didn't you!
S	I'm studying the indigenous people of that particular region of North Africa for my anthropology module at college this term.
E	(to Patsy) Do you want some Bolly, darling?
P	Yeah, just a smidge.
S	It would be really great to go there and study.
E	Study? You don't go to Marrakech to study ...
P	[*catching on*] No, you certainly don't.
E	You go to Marrakech for ... I don't know ... drugs, dirt-cheap plates and rugs ...
P	Yeah ... easygoing sex with gorgeous under-age youths.
E	Yeah ... sex changes, wasn't it, Pats? [*gets a look from Patsy*] Well, not now, not now. So, darling, you don't go there for studying some ingenuous peasants for an anthology module.
S	It would really help with my course ...
P	No, no, no.

Poor

E   Sorry I was so long, darling. I had to clear out my wardrobe, get rid of all these horrible revolting, unfashionable clothes that I simply would not wear, darling, because they are not fashion. I've put them on the floor to throw them out.

M   I thought you'd put them on, dear.

E   What are you doing here?

M   Oh, just thought I'd make the most of the house while you can still afford to keep it up.
[*passage omitted*]

E   Oh, darling, make Mummy a cup of coffee, darling. Would you, sweetie, from the new machine, darling?

M   Oooh, a chappacino.

E   C- A- P- P- U- C- I- N- O . All right. [*to Saffron*] Oh, go on, darling, make the most of Mummy while you're still at home, before you run away to be a student.

M   [*to Saffron*] Oh, you told her, dear. Well done.

E   Oh, God! Although why anybody wants to be a student nowadays is a mystery to me . . .

M   [*to Saffron*] Just jealous, dear.

E   [*reacting*] I could have been a student.

M   Oh-ho-ho. Thick as two short planks, her reports said. [*Saffron goes to the fridge*]

E   It did not say that, it did not say that. Ask Patsy, darling. She wrote most of them.

S   There's no milk.

E   Oh, no milk. Haven't Harrods been here yet, darling. They're normally here by now, aren't they?

S   I'll pop out and get some.

E   Oh, no, that would be a complete waste of money.

S   And how would you know? When was the last time you bought a carton of milk?

E   A carton? Now stop it. Stop getting me all hung-up about money, darling. It's all pounds-shillings-and-pence to me.

S   It was probably the last time you had anything to do with it. The Queen carries more cash. Your whole life is on account.

E   Oh, stop it. I'll have it black, all right.

M   [*to Saffron*] I'll have a black chappaccino, Saffy.

E   [*to Mother*] Espresso.

M   Yes, I am in rather a hurry. As a matter of fact, I think I'd better be off. I want to catch the post.

(Source: BBC Books, 1994)

ACTIVITY 44

The character of each individual is created by their lexical choice, use of collocations and terms of address.

1 Find examples of these in both extracts. You will find little evidence of non-fluency features, hesitations or incomplete clauses but check. Look also for examples of the comic devices listed above. Note too the discourse structure patterning and the topic transitions.

Stand-up comedy

Stand-up comedy is another familiar genre. What is particularly interesting about this comic genre is that although it is pre-planned, and may even be scripted, it must sound spontaneous. Hence normal non-fluency features like fillers, hesitations, false starts, contracted forms and repetitions are often added in performance. To see how this works, we shall look at an extract from the *published text* of a Victoria Wood comic monologue, and compare it with a transcribed extract from a live comic performance.

Extract 6 from 'Bronteburgers'
The speaker is a guide taking visitors round Haworth Parsonage, home of the Brontë family

Right, I'm your official guide. Now before I show you round, I'll just fill you in on a few details, as we call them. As you can see, we're standing in the hall of the Haworth Parsonage, where Haworth's parson, the Reverend Brontë, lived here with his daughters, the famous Brontë sisters, now, alas, no longer with us – but they have left us their novels, which I've not read, being more of a Dick Francis nut. Now, if you pass by me into the parlour (mind my vaccination) ... This is what was known in those days as a parlour, somewhat similar to our lounge-type sitting-room affair in modern terminology. I'm afraid the wallpaper isn't the original period to which we're referring to, it is actually Laura Ashley, but I think it does give some idea of what life must have been like in a blustery old Yorkshire community of long ago. That portrait on the wall is actually of Charlotte Brontë, one of the famous Brontë sisters, and of course to us she may seem a rather gloomy-looking individual; but you must remember these days she'd have a perm, or blusher, or I suppose even drugs would have helped her maintain a more cheerful attitude. In fact she'd probably not be dead if she was alive today.

(Source: Up to You, Porky: The Victoria Wood Sketch Book (1985) Methuen)

Transcript 42: Eddie Izzard performing live
EI covers a number of topics in this show (eg advertising, doing the laundry, auctioneering and in the section below, pets). He walks around the stage as he talks, acting different roles. Audience laughter is so frequent that it has been impossible to signal it. EI also speaks very fast and some passages are virtually inaudible. The transcript starts shortly after he's walked on stage

EI   er hello [*sings a few notes*] so yes well er show time and er actually it's a fairly crap beginning isn't it just walking on and going like this erm I haven't really got anything worked out I really I think if it's West End you really people expecting a huge beginning something like a musical you know 400 people'll be on in the first number ...

[*passage omitted*]

          ... cats and dogs they're very interesting with human beings actually ... they're the only animals and we have pets because they lower our blood pressure ... it's 180 over 60 what does that mean I don't know I'm a dog actually when doctors do that [*take your blood pressure*] ... they've actually got a jumping spider behind your back ... yeah that's what we do it's jumping spider time so yes anyway that's what they do you erm the dog takes your blood pressure and the cat drains all the blood from your body so what you're one of these mobile blood banks so you wake up feeling all anaemic to your cat and dog counting out fivers … the dog's goes *hooooo* the cat's going *pprrrr* because they're drilling aren't they that's what they're doing they're drilling they drill for gold they drill for oil they drill for anything just for the love of drilling when they're behind your sofa they're just drilling they've got goggles on it's OK there's a compressor over there your friends come in they say I think your cat's drilling behind the sofa I don't think so that's purring that noise isn't it cat you drilling the cat hears it whips off its goggles oh no no drilling oh no I'm a cat what would I know how to drill that's purring you're thinking of there yeah purring oh yeah purring good old purr back here not drilling no no not drilling … cat's are much cooler than dogs though aren't they cats have a scam going you buy the food they eat the food they go away you have no control over your cat you can't say to your cat cat heel stay wait lie down roll over your cat'll just be sitting there going just as well you finished …

(*Source:* Unrepeatable, *Ella Communications Ltd/Polygram Video Ltd, 1994*)

The structure of the performance is relatively clear, as **EI** moves smoothly and rapidly from topic to topic. How much elaboration is spontaneous, and how much prepared in advance, is impossible to know. The first few minutes are marked by non-fluency features, incomplete clauses, false starts etc. It is noticeable that once he gets into his stride imaginatively, these features are much reduced. The lengthy development of the joke about the animals' relationship with the owner is likely to have been pre-planned however, particularly the surreal humour of the drilling/purring cat.

ACTIVITY 45

1 Compare the written text of the Wood monologue with the transcribed Izzard performance in terms of narrative structure, non-fluency features, tone, lexical choice and interpersonal features.

2 Choose a stand-up comic whose work you enjoy and select a short session to analyse. Look at the frequency of vague language and non-fluency devices in the data. Compare your findings with other people's analyses of different comics.

News broadcasting

News broadcasting is a public and planned genre. News stories on radio and television are read either from printed text or from a teleprompter to communicate information as clearly and concisely as possible, with photo images added in the case of television news. Selection of news stories and writing the text is the responsibility of the editorial team. As in a newspaper, the possibility of editorial bias is always present, though perhaps less obvious than in proprietor-owned journals like *The Times* and the *Sun*. There may be different styles of presentation – BBC television news is alleged to be slightly more formal than ITV. Radio news can also vary from the impersonal and formal on main bulletins to a more familiar, even homely style on local radio or news summaries. Although the news broadcasts are spoken, they bear little relation to any spoken language we have investigated. They are, in fact, written language read aloud, with some permitted variation appearing through the vocal range (pitch, intonation, accent/pronunciation etc) of the male or female newsreader. There are few other features characteristic of spoken discourse, except some use of contracted forms. One interesting point is the way in which other people's words or opinions are included or embedded in the main news story (eg 'sources close to the government indicate that . . .'), thus implying a different stance to the news item than the person presenting the main story (see Chapter 2 on Goffman's notion of *footing* [ie a speaker's alignment to what he or she is saying]).

In one important aspect, however, news broadcasts reflect everyday talk, and that is because each news item is a *story*. In Chapter 3 we looked at the way people tell stories, jokes and anecdotes to each other, and used Labov's theory of narrative structure (*abstract, orientation, complicating action, evaluation* and *resolution*) as an analytic strategy. You may find it interesting to look at the narrative structure of news stories (certainly the more extended ones) using the same approach. (The death of Princess Diana produced an enormous range of narratives with very different evaluations and resolutions.)

Another interesting feature of news broadcasting today is the additional and increasing use of live reporting from the scene of the news event. In a major event you will expect to hear the original news story (studio based) interspersed with live commentary from one or more reporters on the spot, followed by live or recorded interviews back in the studio with 'expert' commentators, or people with specialist interest in the news event. Live reports and expressions of opinion will sometimes display normal non-fluency features, or may be prepared responses if the event was anticipated. If speakers are responding unprepared to questions from the newscaster in the studio, there may well be overlaps, interruptions and back-channel behaviour as well as hesitations and false starts.

Transcript 43: television news bulletin
The major event being reported is the projected electoral defeat of Chancellor Kohl. Having previously completed a summary of headline stories, the newsreader (NR) now returns to the lead story, the German election. JS (John Simpson) and CW (Caroline Wyatt) are reporting live from Bonn. WH (William Horsley), 'our Europe Correspondent', is commenting on 'the Kohl era' from the studio

NR	The full results won't be known until tomorrow, but the final outcome is not in doubt. The latest projections give Helmut Kohl and the CDU and CSU alliance under 35% of the vote, and Gerhard Schroder STD more than 41%. Although they'll be the biggest party in the new parliament, they'll need support from at least one other, possibly the Greens. Our World Affairs editor John Simpson reports from Bonn
JS	Across Germany the Kohl era came to a quiet end. After 16 years it seemed to be time. In Koblenz and hundreds of places there was none of the expected surge at the polling stations which won Helmut Kohl the last election. This time he said that he wouldn't stay on if the result was a coalition with the left, and

that's exactly what people have voted for, a coalition headed by the left. Tonight as the first exit poll figures came in there was shock and depression at national headquarters in Bonn. People had expected the result to be much closer. When Helmut Kohl arrived to concede defeat they were still in shock. He *is* the CDU who has dominated the party for a quarter of a century. He took the defeat with dignity but to the end it doesn't seem to have occurred to him that he might lose [*passage omitted*] [*signs off 'This is John Simpson in Bonn'*]

NR Tonight's defeat for Chancellor Kohl brings to an end a political career that lasted for more than fifty years. Our Europe correspondent William Horsley looks back over the Kohl era

[*sound of wildly cheering crowds*]

WH German reunification was a personal triumph for Helmut Kohl. As this decade dawned, Kohl's place in history was already safe. A love of power undid him in the end

[*passage omitted*]

NR and Caroline Wyatt joins us now from Bonn. Caroline, Mr Schroder needs to form a coalition to govern. Is that a virtual formality?

CW No. This could be his hardest task of all. It's a bit like a marriage – you have to find the right partner, discuss the issues and make sure that the partnership will work. In Mr Schroder's case it could be that a weakened conservative party would be more to his taste.

(Source: BBC News, 27.9.1998)

COMMENTARY This is a written text being read aloud. You will notice that there is no evidence of any non-fluency features, as predicted. One utterance begins 'and Caroline Wyatt' but this does not necessarily indicate an incomplete sentence. What is interesting is the way that **NR** and **JS** both use contracted forms ('won't, they'll, wouldn't, that's') to make the register more conversational. Similarly **CW** uses colloquial lexis ('a bit like'). Perhaps more interestingly, the whole text, including the several contributions, could be analysed in terms of narrative structure.

ACTIVITY 46

1 Work out the narrative structure of the extract using Labov's narrative stages.
2 Listen to two news broadcasts on BBC radio and local radio on the same day, and compare the idiolect of the news readers and reporters.

Weather forecasting

Weather forecasting is a different kind of planned public speaking with a common GSP but constantly varying content within the semantic field of meteorology. The information which is being communicated is factual and appears to be scripted (ie read from a teleprompter). However, all television weather forecasters, and some radio forecasters (with the exception of the Shipping Forecast), adopt an informal register to communicate factual information (often disagreeable) in a familiar, friendly way. Radio weather forecasting tends to be more detailed, since there is no weather map to follow visually. David Crystal describes successful weather forecasting as 'a mixture of fluent spontaneity, controlled informality and friendly authority' (1995); characteristic linguistic features include meteorological jargon expressions (formulaic phrases like 'deep depression', 'cold front'), colloquial lexis and statistical details ('75% chance of snow').

Transcript 44: television weather forecast (evening)

Forecaster   good evening to you (.) to the south east of England we've had a pretty wet weekend (.) Buckinghamshire was one of the worst affected areas (.) some very heavy rain here (.) High Wycombe catching 53mm of rain in just 24 hours and we can follow that rain through today (.) on Sunday it gradually worked its way towards Bristol then it drifted its way down to the South and into the West (.) still lots of rain around in parts of Northern Ireland and parts of Scotland but the main problem's going to be a lot of low cloud and its going to be a fairly misty night as well (.) even some fog patches in places (.) a blanket of cloud covering most of Britain means that temperatures won't fall any lower than around 9 or 10 degrees Centigrade as now a bit more typically around 11–12 (.) so (.) quite a mild night to come (.) the main problem being those mist patches even some fog patches especially for the hills and mountains (.) on some of those high routes visibility's down to around 100 metres or less (.) so a dull grey damp start for tomorrow morning (.) the brighter weather emerging from the west throughout the day (.) and here we'll start to see through those holes opening in the cloud through the morning (.) and eventually some sunshine coming through (.) but there'll be a lot of cloud around about (.) and down the East coast (.) that cloud it will give some outbursts of rain

COMMENTARY   Weather forecasting is in complete contrast to newscasting, though the task of each is to convey information.

ACTIVITY 47

Look for contrasting use of formulaic phrases, collocations, contracted forms, interpersonal usage, non-fluency features, incomplete clauses and colloquial lexis.

Documentary

Documentary is a public and planned spoken genre, often factually based, whose purpose is to inform, entertain and sometimes persuade an audience. It can be presented through various media, including film, radio and television. The list of documentary techniques is endless: omniscient voiceover, visual images, extracts from texts, taped conversations, recollected conversations, eyewitness accounts or reports, interviews, personal narratives, music, dramatisations, expert views. Predictably, the talking is similarly varied. The brief extract below has been selected as a typical opening of a televised documentary. A narrative voice identifies the subject of the television documentary, and briskly establishes the reason for this choice, before moving on to persuade the viewer of its uniqueness and hinting at exciting new revelations about the subject. A sense of drama is immediately created – the audience is to be captivated by the ideas and associations set up in the first few visual frames and persuaded to stay tuned.

Transcript 45: opening of televised documentary on the country fox

Voice-over   This is the tale of a celebrated predator, the fox. Its urban cousin is easier to see and easier to film. Now for the first time the mysteries of the country fox have been documented, together with one of the animals on which it is most dependent, the rabbit.

Voice 1   Then *Brer Fox* walked out from the bushes and laughed, for this was just what he'd hoped would happen. 'Now I've caught you at last and I mean to punish you. You won't play any more tricks on me.'

Voice-over   From our early childhood . . .

(Source: BBC, 1998)

ACTIVITY 48

The two voices here are interesting: look at the lexical choice in each turn. Note the references to stories and story telling, and the range of comparative forms (including lexis, collocations and grammatical forms). How are these used to involve the audience?

Speaking in public: the lecture

Giving a successful lecture in public is rather like making a speech or scripting a soap opera – you have to make it sound as spontaneous and interpersonal as if you are talking to your audience, not lecturing them, though in fact it will have been carefully planned and scripted. If you read out your planned lecture word for word, the effect on your audience is likely to be soporific. However interesting your material, however well organised your ideas and arguments, they will lose much of their force. David Crystal (1995) quotes the distinguished physicist Sir Lawrence Bragg's comment that reading out one's lecture is 'a terrible thing to do'. Bragg sees 'the spoken word and the written [as] quite different arts', and argues that what justifies bringing together lecturer and audience (who could actually *read* the text) is 'the emotional contact' as the lecturer 'thinks' through his ideas with them, observing and responding to their reactions. Lecturing, according to this view, is like a *dialogue*, with one participant silent (apart from their body language).

We said earlier that the stand-up comic often adds features of spoken language to their script in performance. Lecturers are rather less focused on performance, more on communicating ideas to their audience, and are thus unlikely to add non-fluency features (though these may be present as part of the lecturer's idiolect). Nor is there any obligation for the lecturer to adopt an informal register and colloquial lexis unless it is appropriate to his or her subject. What does seem necessary in a successful lecture is interpersonal language, a reasonable amount of eye contact, as well as a carefully planned and illustrated argument, seemingly effortless, which interests, informs and excites the audience.

Transcript 46: from Michael Halliday's Summer School lecture on basic concepts in systemic functional linguistics

This introductory lecture was addressed to Summer School participants, some of whom were academics in the field of systemic linguistics, others of whom were graduate students

MH Right first of all we have to get the technology going (.) I hate these things because of the kind of feedback you get (.) also (.) I plan to interact with C at certain points and also bring others in so there maybe moments when you you're going to get switched off and in fact I'm just going to try this now (.) test how far my voice carries without too much damage to my throat (.) OK I would be much happier if you don't mind (.) but please if I'm letting the voice drop or anything else is getting in the way do you know stamp your feet or wave or something [*laughter*] I just want to pick on something that R said because I'm really delighted to be here ah very privileged to be here

[*passage omitted*]

now it's it's tempting always on this occasion to try to move in erm to a discussion of a theory kind of historically err I'm not going to do this because it takes too long er it's it's nice but it's lengthy ah and it tends to get full of distractions when you talk about all of the interesting people in the past so all I want to do at this moment and I shall come back to this motif but all I want to do is to emphasise that there is a history (.) Now er now this is not a revolutionary er theory it is er very much part of the post-Saussurian tradition of linguistics in Europe (.) so all these the Indian the Chinese the Greek and slightly later the Arabic er were the classical very strong classical traditions in linguistics and they they are very much part of our heritage and I hope I can say particularly part of our own heritage in systemic work (.) and I think it's important not to lose sight of this because we do need a really rich conceptualisation of language and again I say this with feeling because er I mean there are some very impoverished views of language around er which in one way or another trivialise it (.) there's a constant tendency in the academic world to disengage with language (.) to find excuses for studying anything else (.) right (.) because it's too hard OK so oh no language doesn't matter all you need is this that or the other whatever it is erm the interesting thing is that people who say this always use language to say it [*laughter*] ah and it won't do (.) and one of the things I think that characterises work in the systemic tradition is that those who've used it and developed it er have always been able to look all around them and to say OK (.) I am studying this particular phenomenon (.) maybe in great detail and focusing on this but all the time I'm aware of a perspective from round about (.) will it stand up when I go and move over there and look at language from another angle (.) because if it won't it's no good (.) so we are focusing on language as the primary object of study (.) language as the primary object of study but in order to do that we're going to look from all sides both from within language and from outside and we're going to ask the sorts of questions that people outside ask (.) that teachers ask (.) that clinicians ask (.) that lawyers ask and all that kind of thing (.) that's what we're really on about

(Source: Michael Halliday, 25th International Systemic Functional Summer School and Congress, Cardiff, July 1998)

COMMENTARY   In this introductory lecture **MH** is dealing with the practical aspects of the talk (use of a microphone) before starting on the substance of the lecture. He establishes communication with the audience in practical terms ('if I'm letting the voice drop . . . stamp your feet or wave . . .') and creating a personal rapport. This interpersonal communication is continued by use of features like personal pronouns, interrogatives, even a joke ('people who say this always use language to say it').

ACTIVITY 49

1 Identify key points in the development of the argument. Then look for examples of colloquial lexis, non-fluency features, rhetorical devices, vague language. How effective do you think the full lecture would be? Suggest reasons.

2 You may have access to a variety of lectures. With appropriate permission, record the first and last five minutes of several lectures and compare the use of interpersonal strategies.

3 You have been asked to give a lecture on a subject you know well to a) elderly residents in a nursing home b) your local youth club c) other people interested in the subject d) the local PTA association. Prepare your opening words (about a paragraph of written text) for each audience, and read them out to your group. Compare and discuss different strategies adopted by different members of the group, in the light of possible audience reaction.

6 Case Study: Gendered Talking?

The purpose of this final chapter is to undertake a case study in which we investigate talk, not from the perspective of its planned or unplanned, private or public nature, but focusing rather on the gender of the talkers. Whether the talking takes place in mixed groups (male and female) or in single sex groups (male/male or female/female) the gender of the participants does seem to make a difference. Why this might be so is the subject of our final chapter.

Gender stereotypes in spoken language

Stereotypical ideas about the way gender affects speech are: women gossip, men are strong and silent; women talk about domestic and personal trivia; men talk about important topics (business, money, the government); women have soft and gentle voices or alternatively have loud, strident voices; women screech whilst men have rich, deep, reassuring tones conveying confidence and authority – the list is endless. However, we encounter innumerable contradictions to these stereotypes on a daily basis. By the end of this chapter we may be closer to understanding the reasons for this difference between stereotype and actual usage.

Theoretical approaches to gender and spoken language

Over the past twenty years, sociolinguists have been investigating the effects of gender on language, and have focused in particular on gender and spoken language (though there is also interest in gender and written language).

Jennifer Coates (1993) identifies two approaches which she describes as *dominance* and *difference*.

Dominance

The dominance approach 'sees women as an oppressed group, and interprets differences in women's and men's speech in terms of men's dominance and women's subordination'. Researchers and theorists taking this view include Robin Lakoff (1975), Dale Spender (1980) and Zimmerman and West (1983).

Difference

The difference approach sees women and men as belonging to 'different sub-cultures', who are differently socialised from childhood onwards, and who may therefore have different problems in communication as adults. Deborah Tannen (1989) is an exponent of this position.

Power and powerlessness

Deborah Cameron in *Verbal Hygiene* (1995) argues that theorists like Lakoff and Spender see gendered language in terms of power and powerlessness for this reason: throughout Western culture the masculine/male has been the *unmarked norm* in language, the feminine/female the *marked* form. Since markedness is regarded as a deviation from the norm, the clear assumption must be that power lies in the unmarked or masculine/male form. For example, we have the unmarked forms 'manager', 'usher' and 'Paul' and the marked forms 'manager*ess*', 'usher*ette*', and 'Paul*ine*'. Furthermore, Tannen's views (1990) identify gender differences in terms of competitiveness (male) and co-operation (female).

Cameron *challenges* the whole idea that there are two different and contrasting languages for men and women, arguing that this is a *defecit model* approach (one language is inferior to the other). She asks whether gender alone is at the core of individual identity – is the term genderlect more precise or less than idiolect?

The way women (or men, or men and women) talk in a variety of situations (casual conversation, service encounters, occupational contexts etc) may reveal the effects of disempowerment, or may signal the effects of other variables, including socio-economic status, education, context, peer group, even personality. The question is – does gender difference *override* these other variables, or is it *overridden*? We may be closer to an answer after we have investigated the data below.

Gender and casual conversation

The genre of this data is casual conversation between friends of different sexes, where talking seems least affected by consciousness of gender difference, and to be most relaxed. As we have seen, characteristics of casual conversation include adjacency pairs, vague language, non-fluency features, topic and speaker shift, back-channel behaviour, politeness markers, overlaps, interruptions and other strategies for retaining speaker control. Even silence in casual conversation can have a function; refusal to participate can be a control strategy, or it may be an expression of disempowerment.

Gender, grammar and lexis

Researchers have investigated men's and women's use of spoken language in casual conversation and discovered substantial evidence that men interrupt women even when women are of higher status; that they hold the floor longer, and take longer turns; that they tend to reject women's topic choice and prefer their own (though women are willing to talk about men's topics).

Men use imperatives as directives; they use stronger swear words (see Transcript 47) and a higher proportion of slang and colloquial lexis (look at Transcripts 49, 50 and 51); they use more hypotaxis (embedded structures) in the sentence, whilst women use more parataxis (linked structures). Women allegedly use more intensifiers ('terribly', 'awfully', 'so', 'very'), more evaluative lexis (communicating feelings and attitudes) and more politeness markers ('please', 'thank you'); they initiate exchanges more than men; they use more back-channel behaviour including minimal responses, and will use 'yeah' and 'I see' to keep communication going (look at Transcript 47); they use declaratives, rising intonation, tag questions and multiple modality in directives or compound requests; their sentences are more often incomplete than men's; they make more use of diminutives in terms of address (Lizzie, Rosie, Freddy) or reduplications ('teeny-weeny', 'itsy-bitsy') or pet names ('Pooh'); they use more euphemism than men, use weaker swear words and less often (look at Transcripts 47 and 48); they use less slang and colloquial language and more first person pronouns.

Gender and discourse strategies

Women tend to use more simultaneous speech (especially in same-sex exchanges), and are able to overlap each other co-operatively, without producing conversation malfunction or miscommunication; they apologise more to ensure social harmony and support the 'other' (men apologise if they really have to, but prefer to avoid such face-threatening acts). Women pay compliments as positive politeness strategies (men insult each other to show affectionate solidarity; they compliment women but tend to reinforce their subordinate status); women use more hedges ('kind of', 'sort of', 'I think'), more end tags ('and stuff', 'something like that') and more adjectives of approximation ('about', 'around'). Women use more standard forms and prestige accents (with exceptions); they facilitate and support conversational fluency and avoid face-threatening situations, whereas men allegedly do the opposite (eg Transcripts 47, 48 and 49).

Men and women talking

The data below consists of extracts from six transcripts of mixed and same sex casual conversations. Transcripts 47–49 were made by an A-Level English Language student who recorded herself and two close friends (**F1**, **M** and **F2**) in conversation. The transcribed extracts are taken from later in the recording, when the researcher was no longer aware of the tape-recorder, thus avoiding the Observer's Paradox. The fourth transcript is of two women talking about the differences they perceive between talking to women and talking to men. Transcripts 51 and 52 (all male/male exchanges of different ages and in different contexts) are taken from Janet Holmes's study *Women, Men and Politeness* (1995).

Transcript 47: Male and Female
M and F1 are discussing an embarrassing friend

M	the worst thing (.) I can possibly see (.) the nightmare scenario (.) is seeing S— (.) who is in full flow
F1	yes
M	he's like (.) I— (.) shit no (.) you're having a serious conversation with somebody for about fifteen … twenty minutes (.) this (.) suddenly there's this brrrr (.) f****** hell (.) I— (.) arms around you (.) almost knocking you to the floor (.) like just f****** dribbly mess (.) f****** hell (.) there's a girl down there … she definitely wants me … yeah
F1	(laughs) he doesn't does he
M [ ]	no it has been known (.) sort of thing happened before
F1 [ ]	yes it has been known … yeah
M	it's just evil cos (.) it's just so embarrassing when you're just stood talking to somebody (.) people just think who's that w***** (.) f*** (.) I've never seen him before must be off his head (.) pretend you don't know him
F1	yeah … cos … like (.) it's always the same at A— (.) he's everywhere (.) even when … even … even … if … if even (.) when you go downstairs (.) he's always in (.) he's always in with everything isn't he (.) you know how like M— yeah all the time (.) M— yeah (.) M— (.) M— and V— are into everything aren't they (.) no matter where they are (.) they're into (.) if there's something there they're into (.) they'll be into it (.) you know what I mean (.) they're into this

[*passage omitted*]

F1	it is listen right (.) C— and M— used to hang around with each other (.) yeah

(.) it used to be C— was just there (.) the big head and M— would be the little movement of the duo

M yeah (.) but C— would just like (.) go like … yeah … But M— won't do anything in front of hundreds of people (.) if people will (.) C— will make people stand around and watch him and he'll make sure people watch him (.) whereas if people stopped and turned round and looked at M— (.) M— would just like go errm aha

F1 yeah

M it's got to be like three or four people who he's actually talking to

F1 yeah

M then like a couple of people who've just turned their heads (.) whereas like if people stood around in like … like in a little semi-circle like they are with C— every (.) everyone gives him a bit of room because they know suddenly he's just going to go waaa and people will go flying everywhere (.) it's like it's different it's like …

F1 [*laughs*] yeah I think M—'s like that cos every time you (.) everywhere you look in progress you see M— going (.) just doing something

M yeah (.) it's like (.) that's (.) that's what I'm saying (.) he can do it when there's only like (.) if there's a small audience C— can perform to an enormous audience

F1 yeah … I know

M it's got to be small or else he'll have (.) he'll get shy and doesn't do anything else

F1 do you reckon

M [ ] he does (.) especially if there's loads of people he doesn't know very well (.) unless of course he's completely out of his mind

F1 in which case he just becomes it

M yeah he just becomes too big

F1 he comes (.) he comes C— triple (.) he dances on picnic benches on M— Park

(Source: Karen Dell)

ACTIVITY 50

1 Referring to the research findings above, list the features characterising:
  a casual conversation
  b women's speech.
2 Compare list **a** and list **b** and note the frequency of occurrence of each feature common to both. What features only occur in list **a** or list **b**? Can you make any deductions about the differences between women's spoken language and the language of casual conversation.

Transcript 48: Female 1 and Female 2

This transcript is on the *Living Language Cassette* as 'Investigating Talk Extract 7'. The cassette version extends this transcript by several minutes.

The speakers are discussing plans for going out with a group of friends

F1 … and she goes do you want to come and I said yeah (.) def … definitely want to come and everything and erm (.) she wasn't going to take her car but she's taking her car up now and erm (.) N— (.) N—'s going erm (.) D—'s going (.) S—'s going (.) what's— S—'s girlfriend

F2 L—

F1 L—'s going erm (.) N—'s going (.) wow … and erm

F2 K—

F1 K—'s not going (.) I think that's it so far (.) but she had to (.) said she (.) she

had to go and see (.) see M— or something and erm (.) how ... how come
you're not going

F2   I er I might be (.) I don't know
F1   cos she can (.) I reckon she can fit you into her car cos I reckon it's just me ...
      N— me and N— in the car (.) cos ...
F2 [ ] we've done it before haven't we
F1   yeah cos she (.) cos ... cos in D—'s car all those lot I've just said are going in
      that and
F2 [ ] oh right (.) how much is it then
F1   er (.) ten quid (.)
F1   [S—] doesn't know if she's going out or not but I personally reckon that she
      will
F2   yeah (.) I'll have a word with M— tomorrow (.) he'll go cos it's like ten quid (.)
      whereabouts is it (.) Leeds
F1   yeah (.) we'll have to give her some money as well for her petrol
F2   yeah
F1   cos I'm trying to work out how much to give her cos (.) cos she's driven us up
      to Milton Keynes
F2   I know (.) shall we give her something like three quid
F1   what for
F2   or four quid
F1   for all of them (.) I was on about giving her a tenner
F2   oh were you
F1   yeah
F2   yeah do whatever
F1   or give her a tenner between us cos it looks better then doesn't it
F2   yeah
F1   we'll say we'll give you a tenner now and then next time we'll give
F2 [ ] or we'll just sort her out or something
F1   yeah because erm (.) I was thinking (.) Milton Keynes
F2   I know
F1   and ... and G— yeah (.) cos I said (.) I said the other (.) last time I saw her I
      was going to give her some money for then like but that was then like sort of
      thing
F2   yeah
F1   so now this is another time I thought I'd just give her a tenner or something (.)
      cos four (.) three quid looks crap when N— and M— were giving her like
      twenty (.) ten quid and stuff (.) looks sad (.) so I don't know (.) I said to her
      you and M— might be going to R— and she said (.) yeah (.) I know (.) but I
      (.) I thought why (.) what's the point
F2   yeah
F1   cos no-one else is there
[*passage omitted*]

(Source: Karen Dell)

The interesting feature about this transcript is the relationship between the speakers. Does one speaker dominate? If so, how does she establish and sustain dominance in the conversational exchanges? Find evidence to support your view in the data.

Transcript 49: Male, Female 1 and Female 2
The speakers are talking about people's touchiness

M	errr (.) it's not (.) it's not what you do (.) it's the way you say it (.) there's nothing you can really do (.) do to D— apart from perhaps (.) trying to think what you can to do to D—(.) err
F1	his clothes
F2	oh yeah (.) definitely
M	yeah but that's just (.) that's just joking weren't it (.) you mean how you can nastily f*** someone up (.) make somebody not speak to you for the rest of the night
F1	yeah yeah
M	oh ermm
F2	especially B—
M	with B— it's anything (.) B— (.) I mean if you get (.) if you want to get (.) if you want to get him to not speak to you for the rest of the night and risk getting smacked in the mouth you can say
F1 [ ]	why (.) is he (.) is he a bit hard
M	well (.) he … he … er (.) I don't know (.) I don't (.) I don't (.) I don't know (.) I suppose he is really but like (.) there's certain things you don't say because you know you get some sort of violent response if you do
F1	yeah
M	well you might get some sort of violent response like if you turn (.) if you (.) nobody's actually said this to him and not got hit cos I've only ever heard one person say it to him and they got immediately smacked
F1 [ ]	well (.) who (.) who's said it to him
M	this lad called J— W— (.) he's in (.) who (.) who's two years younger than us =
F1 [ ]	yeah
M =	says to him (.) have you noticed B—'s got a mole on his forehead
F1	yes (.) I know
F2	yeah (.) a spot there
F1	the thing is right (.) the thing is right (.) every time (.) you know when B— (.) we first like used to go out with you lot (.) D— and M— and everyone (.) B— suddenly became new (.) cos like yeah
F2 [ ]	yeah
F1	for months and weeks and weeks (.) everyone talked about B— (.) we never actually met B—
M [ ]	it were (.) it was cos he never used to come out
F2	yeah (.) and then one day we had a get-together round L—'s (.) loads of people there (.) and erm (.) it happened for er (.) well (.) till everyone actually got to know B— (.) well (.) not actually everyone does yet (.) as they were getting to (.) like people would come round like M— and stiff (.) and people like (.) someone (.) I don't know (.) J— the er … people just kept appearing and disappearing (.) and each time a new person arrived (.) as in someone that was new to B— and B— wasn't in the room someone would say (.) where's B— and they'd say (.) which one's that (.) is that the one with the mole between his eyebrows
F1	oh no
F2	someone would say it
[passage omitted]	
M	just (.) just like he said (.) just grabbed hold of him (.) threw him down and said (.) don't you f****** say that (.) anything like that to me again and just like smacked him

(Source: Karen Dell)

ACTIVITY 52

Working in small groups, read aloud this transcript two or three times, trying to make it sound as 'real' as possible. Each individual or grouping (whatever is most convenient) should select one of the speakers (**F1**, **F2** or **M**) for detailed study. Differentiate and describe the characteristic idiolect of each speaker, noting (for example) their use of non-fluency features, length of turn, lexical choice and use of overlaps and interruptions.

Transcript 50: Women talking about male/female conversations

*The speakers are **M** (Meg) and **B** (Bea). Meg is explaining how talking with her male partner is different from talking with her female friend*

M   it [*talk with Mike*] never kind of develops in the way that say it does wi- wi- with say Bea ... and nevertheless we say the same sort of thing, the same type of way, but somehow it doesn't have – I don't know how you're gonna work this one out, Jennifer, cos I'm sure this is quite an important and subtle difference, but I wouldn't know how to describe it. Would you Bea?

B   No. I think I know what you mean that – it – that the men don't get into it to such an extent and carry it on. They kind of listen to what you have to say and sort of say, 'Yes that does sound bad' or something, and it doesn't go – it doesn't go much further ...

M   Yeah. One of the differences is – is that they don't mirror it. I think that's really an important difference because I mean Mike will listen patiently and interestedly and concernedly to – to various things that I have to talk about, but he doesn't make those kind of – I mean like you and I have – I mean I – I'm – I'm always aware of the kind of *balanced* um – the *balance* that comes into conversation between two women, between two friends

B   mhm

M   and um you just don't get that in my experience with a man

[*later Meg describes some other difference*]

M   I always find that men will say, 'Oh it's differerent'. They're – they look for the differences between your experiences rather than the similarities. Like my brother, and he's in the army, and say if we're talking about interviewing, um I say, 'Well I had to interview all these people', and he'll say, 'Oh well we interview in the army', and I'll say 'Well, isn't it amazing how so and so', and he'll say, something like, 'Oh well it's different', you know, 'We have a set interview room' – um but there ARE elements that are the same but he – he always looks for the difference and so does Mike.

(Source: Coates, 1996)

ACTIVITY 53

In this transcript the speakers are describing what they think are the differences between men and women talking together.

1 Construct a short questionnaire to find out what a range of respondents (different age and gender) think are the differences between male and female talk.

2 Compare your findings with the suggested differences identified in this chapter.

Transcript 51: men talking to men

The speakers are young men working in a bakery; they are discussing what apples are packed in

Ray   crate
Sam   case
Ray   what
Sam   they come in cases Ray not crates
Ray   oh same thing if you must be picky over every one thing
Sam   just shut your f****** head Ray
Ray   don't tell me to f*** off f*** (...)
Sam   I'll come over and shut yo
Jim   [*laughingly using a thick sounding voice*] yeah I'll have a crate of apples thanks
Ray   no f*** off Jim
Jim   a dozen
Dan   [*amused*] s*** picker

(Source: Holmes, 1995)

Transcript 52: three male/male apologies

Student and professor
Michael   Sorry we're late. We got stuck in the lift
Professor   Michael you're always late
Michael   Sorry Prof. I promise I'll be early next time
Professor   I'll believe it when I see it

Friend phoning friend to cancel a lunch date
Joe   I'm sorry I can't make it after all. I've got an unexpected meeting. It's a real pain
Sam   Let's make another time

Male waiter to male chef in restaurant
Chef   Don't take that
Waiter   Sorry I thought it was ready to go
Chef   Don't take anything till I say
Waiter   Sorry
Chef   [*says nothing*]

(Source: Holmes, 1995)

ACTIVITY 54

Using the data in Transcripts 51 and 52 and any other relevant data elsewhere in the book (eg telephone language in Chapter 3), identify as many features as possible which seem to characterise male/male informal conversation.

Gender and spoken language studies – the future?

So much research is going on internationally in the field of gender and spoken language that new findings appear all the time. A recent collection of articles (ed. Coates, 1998) demonstrates the range and variety of current research, including an investigation of separate male and female dialects in an Australian Aboriginal language, sex differences in adolescent speech, politeness strategies in Mexico and New Zealand, as well as studies of gendered speech among physicians and police officers. The more evidence is amassed, the clearer the overall picture will be, as patterns emerge about the effects of socialisation, education, workplace and leisure environments on men and women as they talk their way through life. What is becoming clear is that though sexual politics remains a crucial factor in explaining male and female ways of talking, it is not the only consideration. The *dominance* model confirmed that differences exist between men and women, located these differences within a contextual framework of power or lack of power, identified differing linguistic features, commented on the socialisation of boys and girls in the same patriarchal tradition – but ultimately provided a description rather than a solution. The *difference* model offered explanations for and interpretations of male/female miscommunication, but seemed to propose no alternative strategies for rectifying these misunderstandings other than understanding them. Since women are apparently more worried about these problems, their solution would appear to be – if you can't beat them, join them. The *deficit* model even identified 'women's language' as an inferior version of men's.

All three models offer alternative descriptions or explanations of the *status quo* rather than proposing any way forward. Current researchers are looking ahead in their investigations of gender, sex and sexuality issues, and linking them to sociology, education, demography and neurology studies. Important questions are being asked, all of which have implications for language and gender studies. Does biological difference affect brain function? Are people rigidly sexed as male/female? Why are girls outperforming boys at school? What effect does socialisation have upon sexual or gender identity? How should we regard intersexed individuals (people whose sexual identity is congenitally indeterminate)?

Perhaps we need to re-visit stereotypical assumptions about the effects of biological difference and early gendered socialisation on an individual. If economic, educational and occupational opportunities become readily available, reversing historical trends towards patriarchy (or, occasionally, matriarchy), then gender could be regarded as one of *many* variables affecting the way we talk. It is only in cultures where *social inequity and gender are directly linked* that language mirrors gender difference in a negative way. (Hence the development of the dominance, difference and deficit models.) If the language which men or women use, talking together or talking to each other, suits the speakers and their purposes, then gender difference is irrelevant. As we have seen throughout this book, successful private talking depends on speakers being co-operative, adaptable, sensitive to other speakers' needs and adhering to the conversational maxims. Successful public talking, whether planned or unplanned, also needs to adhere broadly to the conversational maxims, but on a continuum which may range from co-operation to competitiveness, depending on the context, purpose and participants. Neither in public or private talk is the gender identity of the participants necessarily significant. Rather than asking the question – why do men and women speak differently? – the better question is – how do people manage to speak so differently in so many different situations and circumstances? As Bing and Bergvall suggest (1996, cited in Coates, 1998), continuing to polarise gendered language into fixed boundaries ignores the reality of male/female discourse today, where we encounter 'a complicated network of criss-crossing intersecting similarities and differences'. We need to accept this diversity, rather than trying to force it back into gender categories. Instead of alternating between the deficit, dominance and difference models to describe gendered talking today, a better and more precise term might be the *diversity* model. Using such a model enables difference in spoken language to be recognised, investigated and theorised across the gender divide. Since the most remarkable characteristic of talk is its predictable unpredictability, any model which defines and celebrates this diversity is more than welcome.

Suggested reading

Chapter 1

Jean Aitchison, *Words in the Mind* (1987) Blackwell.

Jean Aitchison, *The Seeds of Speech* (1996) Cambridge University Press.

David Crystal, *The Cambridge Encyclopaedia of Language* (1987) Cambridge University Press.

Robin Dunbar, *Grooming, Gossip and the Evolution of Language* (1996) Faber and Faber.

Michael Halliday, *Learning How to Mean* (1975) Arnold.

Frank Myszor, *Living Language: Language Acquisition* (1999) Hodder & Stoughton.

Steven Pinker, *The Language Instinct* (1994) Penguin.

Colin Renfrew, *Archaeology and Language* (1987) Penguin.

Chapter 2

David Crystal, *The Cambridge Encyclopaedia of Language* (1987) Cambridge University Press.

David Nunan, *Introducing Discourse Analysis* (1993) Penguin.

Christine Cheepen and James Monaghan, *Spoken English: A Practical Guide* (1990) Pinter.

Ronald Carter and Michael McCarthy, *Exploring Spoken English* (1997) Cambridge University Press.

Chapter 3

David Crystal, *The Cambridge Encyclopaedia of Language* (1987) Cambridge University Press.

Janet Maybin and Neil Mercer (ed.), *Using English: From Conversation to Canon* (1996) The Open University and Routledge.

Chapter 4

Adrian Beard, *The Language of Sport* (1998) Routledge.

Ronald Carter and Michael McCarthy, *Exploring Spoken English* (1997) Cambridge University Press.

Hywel Coleman (ed.), *Working with Language: A Multi-disciplinary Consideration of Language Use in Work Contexts* (1989) Mouton de Gruyter.

Chapter 5

Allan Bell, *The Language of News Media* (1991) Blackwell.

Sharon Goodman and David Graddol (eds), *Redesigning English: New texts, new identities* (1996) Routledge.

Janet Maybin and Neil Mercer, *Using English: from conversation to canon* (1996) Routledge.

P. Scannell, *Broadcast Talk* (1991) Sage.

Chapter 6

Deborah Cameron (ed), *The Feminist Critique of Language* (1990) Routledge.

Jennifer Coates and Deborah Cameron, *Women in their Speech Communities* (1989) Longman.

Jennifer Coates, *Women, Men and Language*, 2nd edn (1993) Longman.

Jennifer Coates, *Women Talk* (1996) Blackwell.

Jennifer Coates (ed), *Language and Gender: A Reader* (1998) Blackwell.

David Graddol and Joan Swann, *Gender Voices* (1989) Blackwell.

Janet Holmes, *Women, Men and Language* (1995) Longman.

Sara Mills (ed), *Language and Gender: Interdisciplinary Perspectives* (1995) Longman.

Cate Poynton, *Language and Gender: Making the Difference* (1985) Oxford University Press.

Deborah Tannen, *You Just Don't Understand: Women and Men in Conversation* (1990) Virago.